# PRAISE FOR **HELLO, NAUSEA. HOW ARE YOU TODAY?**

In *Hello, Nausea. How Are You Today?* Julie Shaw takes the reader through an intimate, personal journey of her diagnosis, treatment, and ultimately, recovery from breast cancer. She skillfully weaves her own physical, emotional, and cognitive reactions and responses with humor, wisdom, and practical suggestions that will be useful for anyone going through a difficult diagnosis and treatment. Julie draws from her extensive knowledge and experience of yoga and yoga therapy, making this book a treasure for anyone interested in learning how to help themselves, or others, on the journey of healing and recovery.

Gary Kraftsow, MA, C-IAYT, Founder and Director,
American Viniyoga Institute

*Hello Nausea. How Are You Today?* is a handbook of yoga wisdom and the author's own healing that informs and inspires. Julie is open and honest in sharing her experience. I wish her book had been available when colleagues and I did breast cancer research in 2017. I would have given it to all the women and doctors who were part of the study. We tried to explain to the doctors that just noticing how one felt at a particular time was doing yoga, but they thought yoga was only poses, and could be practiced most days while on chemo. As the book explains so well, other yoga tools, such as breathing and mindfulness, could be used daily, but on many days physical movement/āsana were not possible or wanted. Julie's book demonstrates the significance of tuning in to how one feels, and the importance of keeping a record like a journal, during treatment. She includes at the end of most chapters ways that family and friends might be part of a person's treatment experience. This is the perfect book for all who encounter cancer.

Susan Tebb, PhD, MSW, C-IAYT, RYT-500

This book is an excellent resource for anyone with a cancer diagnosis, in particular, breast cancer. The personal nature of the book can help anyone deepen their understanding of the "whole-person" impact of having cancer, undergoing treatments, and thriving in recovery. The expertly designed and highly relevant yoga therapy practices offer management strategies for a variety of physical, physiological, mental, and emotional symptoms. Julie's sense of humor, honest reflection, and willingness to share her journey is a gift to people with cancer, supportive friends and family, yoga therapists, and yoga teachers.

Mary Hilliker, RDN, E-RYT 500, C-IAYT,
Certified Viniyoga Teacher & Yoga Therapist

Julie Shaw is an informed, gentle, and kind guide through the cancer journey—truly, the best, knowledgeable friend you want by your side. Throughout the generous sharing of her own story of breast cancer, from biopsy to surgery to chemo and radiation, she weaves in yogic wisdom and simple practices that helped her and can help you or a loved one. Her tone throughout is candid and patient. I can't recommend this book highly enough - from its practical discussions about different therapies to spiritual guidance on ways to move through the world. I plan to give this book to any friend or family member who receives a cancer diagnosis, and as a cancer survivor myself, am grateful Julie has shared so generously.

Donna Baier Stein, Award-winning author and
Publisher, Tiferet Journal

This book is beautifully written. It has a conversational, even intimate quality that makes you feel a friend is gently giving you advice during a hard time. There is no preaching, no stridency. It is so useful for someone going through cancer. It also reminded me of the importance of nonattachment and having a comprehensive guide for making the principles of yoga part of my everyday life. I read the book before I knew the outcome of a recent medical scare, and it made me feel confident that, no matter what the results, I'd be able to navigate it.

Susan Lewis, lifelong friend

# HELLO, NAUSEA. HOW ARE YOU TODAY?

Julie Shaw, MEd, C-IAYT

Visit **WindingPathYoga.com** to contact Julie for personal yoga therapy and to find guided instructions through the practices contained in this book.

Published by Gatekeeper Press
7853 Gunn Hwy., Suite 209
Tampa, FL 33626
www.GatekeeperPress.com

Foreword: ©Gary Kraftsow 2024

Photography: Kate Wark Photography

Cover Design, Interior illustration: Robin Locke Monda

Interior Formatting by KUHN Design Group | kuhndesigngroup.com

Copyright © 2025 by Julie Shaw

First edition 2025

ISBN (paperback): 9798990957107
eISBN: 9798990957114

*For Mom and Nana, who showed me strength.*

*For Michael and Emma, who inherited it.*

## CAUTIONS

This book is meant to share my personal journey through cancer treatment, using yoga as a means to aid in self-care. Nothing in this account or the practices described here are suggested as a substitute for professional healthcare or recommended as a specific treatment plan for any condition.

If you have received a cancer diagnosis or are currently in treatment for cancer, discuss with your healthcare provider how the gentle practices in this book might support your care plan.

# CONTENTS

# FOREWORD

Our human system is multidimensional, including our functional anatomy and physiology; our minds, including sensations, perceptions, emotions, feelings, and thoughts; and that more mysterious dimension which, for lack of a universally agreed-upon name, can be thought of as the part of us that is beyond our body and mind—our spirit or soul.

Each of these dimensions has its own functions and potentials, as well as challenges and sources of suffering. Though we can think of each of these dimensions as distinct, they are, in fact, all interrelated. In contemporary healthcare, this interrelated nature of the human system is being recognized more and more, evidenced by the emergence of the field of integrative medicine. Of course, most healthcare providers are trained to focus on one or another dimension and, within dimensions, they may specialize even further.

The Ancients of many cultures recognized this multidimensional nature millennia ago. In Vedic India, the fields of *Āyurveda* (the ancient Vedic medical system) and *Yoga Citiksa* (yoga therapy) evolved. While *Āyurvedic* physicians treat individuals with specific conditions, yoga therapists draw on the multidimensional system of practices devised by the ancient yoga masters, adapting and calibrating them to help clients manage the symptoms they are challenged with as a result of their condition and, more often than not, their treatments. The different practices of yoga focus on and work with specific dimensions of the human system, but were designed to work in an integrated way to address the practitioner's whole being. For those individuals facing the challenge of a difficult diagnosis and treatment protocol, these practices empower them to manage their unique collection of symptoms and limitations in an effective and integrated way.

Among the many conditions that impact the human system, one of the most challenging, yet common, is cancer. Though there are many different kinds and degrees of cancer and different treatment protocols, one consistent reality is their multidimensional impact. While licensed healthcare practitioners are essential, learning what you can do through your own efforts to improve, or at least manage, your symptoms can be life-changing.

In *Hello, Nausea. How Are You Today?* Julie Shaw gives a first-hand account of how she skillfully navigated the challenges of her personal journey through the diagnosis and treatment of cancer, drawing on her own extensive training, deep understanding, and practical experience of yoga and yoga therapy. This book offers the reader both inspiration and practical tips about how they too can manage their own condition, or support loved ones facing their own journey through diagnosis and treatment on the road to recovery. The exercises contained in this book are simple, straightforward, and accessible. They will benefit anyone, with or without prior experience practicing yoga.

**Gary Kraftsow, MA, C-IAYT, E-RYT 500**
*Founder, American Viniyoga Institute*
*California, August 2024*

# PREFACE

Dear Reader,

Thank you for choosing this book. Based on the title, I'm guessing you picked it up because you or someone you know has cancer.

When I was diagnosed with breast cancer, my brain began accepting information on a "need-to-know" basis. I guess I was afraid to find out too much. My wiser self knew that knowledge is power and can help dispel fear, but I found it hard to dive into self-help books and cancer texts. In fact, I read only one book, a cancer memoir, given to me in a gift basket by a small group of friends. The book was called *Laughing All the Way* by Juliana M. Steele.[1]

It was a nice coincidence that the author and I share a similar name—mine is Julie Ann.

I sat down with the book on my sun porch one morning and found myself still there late in the day when I turned the last page. I didn't learn everything there is to know about cancer treatment (and I didn't want to!), but I did learn a few things that really helped me. I learned the differences between the two chemo drugs I would receive; how using ice packs on hands and feet during chemo can salvage the nails; and that the author continued to exercise vigorously through her entire treatment. And I learned that she made a few big decisions about her treatment by defining her own priorities first, then weighing pros and cons before coming to a conclusion, an inspiring and reassuring display of personal agency that I remembered later on when I had my own decisions to make.

Julianna's story gave me a big-picture sense of the cancer treatment journey, albeit from one person's perspective. That scale of information suited me. It was exactly the dose I could handle at the moment, and it helped spur my own inner power as I started down the same path.

My natural starting place to prepare for cancer treatment was through my yoga practice. Yoga itself hasn't changed my life or made me who I am. Instead, it has provided me with a wonderful set of tools to make those changes myself. This book includes stories about what I went through in my treatment and the yoga practices I used to cope with the resulting symptoms.

Each chapter ends with a section called *How Yoga Helped.* Here you'll find exercises, practices, or reflections I used for specific symptoms like post-surgery discomfort, nausea, anxiety, depression, constipation, fatigue, postradiation fibrosis, and others. You can read the book straight through and follow the progression I used, or look in Chapter 22 or in the index for your specific needs. You don't have to be an experienced yogi to use the tools presented here, and there's no need to do all the practices. Take whatever inspiration you find and adapt the practices to meet your personal needs. You don't need special clothes or equipment. In a few cases, a yoga mat will certainly help for exercises that require traction for hands or feet, or to provide cushioning on a hard surface, but often you just need a comfortable spot on the floor or your bed. These practices are meant to be adapted by you, wherever you are and whatever you're wearing. Most days I did my go-to practice in my pajamas, and I still do! There's no single right way to do the exercises—there's only your way.

If you picked up this book for a friend or loved one who has cancer and currently has little energy for digesting a self-help book, I believe it can still be useful. Why not read it yourself first and lead your friend through a few of the exercises? Or help your loved one develop their own personalized practice. That head start might enable them to read the book later on and learn more. It's a small thing you can do that will be a huge help for that dear person. As a special friend and colleague of mine said, "You don't have to move a mountain for the person with cancer; just show them how to move a pebble that day."

Finally, if you have no interest in yoga, you probably would never have picked up this book in the first place! But maybe a friend gave it to you, like my friends gave me the one I read. If that's the case, just change the title in your mind to *Things That Helped Me Get Through Cancer*. It's not the yoga that matters. The point is self-care, finding things that will help you and, hopefully, inspire you to keep moving toward restored health. Going through cancer treatment takes a great deal of energy. Unfortunately, it also *saps* most of our energy! If you can find a few tips that work for you, whether at a superficial level or deeply within your heart, take advantage. That's what this book is about.

Wishing you good health, happiness, and joy,

**Julie Shaw**
*Ridgefield, Connecticut, 2024*

# WHAT IS YOGA, ANYWAY?

Yoga was the tool I used to get through cancer treatment, because that's what I had experience with. There are many "schools" of yoga, and the one I follow is called *Viniyoga*.[1]

This tradition is known specifically for adapting a yoga practice to meet the individual's needs, and you'll see this reflected in **"How Yoga Helped"** sections at the end of each chapter.

But many people don't know what yoga is, beyond seeing images portrayed in the media. Here's a brief perspective:

The word *yoga* comes from the same root as the words *unite* and *yoke*. The things being united, or yoked together, are the various aspects of a human being. One approach to this concept is called the *Pañcamaya* Model (pronounced *PUN-cha MY-a* — *pañca* means *five* and *maya* means *pervade*). It refers to five aspects of our humanity, including:

- **Anatomical:** the structural parts of our body (muscles, bones, fascia, nerves, organs)

- **Physiological/energetic:** our inner systems which operate through exchanges of energy (respiratory, circulatory, nervous, endocrine, etc.)

- **Mental/cognitive:** our capacity to learn from information taken in through our senses by engaging with the external world; learning, memory, attention

- **Intellectual:** our personality or character, formed from "nature and nurture;" the part of us that holds our values, priorities, and sense of right and wrong

- **Inner heart:** our capacity to engage in relationships, to experience pure joy and unconditional love; the core of who we truly are.

In the yoga tradition, these aspects are described as pervading each other, rather than being distinct. An experience affecting one aspect will affect all the others. In other words, we are "whole" beings.

You'll see the graphic in Figure 1 (see next page) representing the *Pañcamaya* model, or what I'll call the Five Aspects Model, at the start of each "How Yoga Helped" section. The graphic is a reminder that no matter what part of us we intend to treat with our yoga practice, the practice will always affect our whole self.

Our Western medical system is often faulted for not treating the whole person. I don't believe it's that simple, although it is true that our system tends to segment healthcare, with different doctors treating different aspects. Yoga also deals with individual aspects, but with the overall objective of reuniting them. But how exactly does that work?

Most people associate yoga with stretching exercises, the physical movements done at the anatomical level. But there are other tools in the yoga toolbox, like breath control, deep relaxation, positive imagery, chanting, and meditation, all of which can help integrate our aspects or layers. It requires focused attention to use these tools in concert, to call on all of our faculties at the physical, mental, and emotional levels. Indeed, attention is a fundamental aspect of yoga. As my yoga teacher[2] says, yoga practice both requires focus and subsequently builds focus.

In simple terms, we could say yoga is a technology, a set of tools, specifically designed to train our

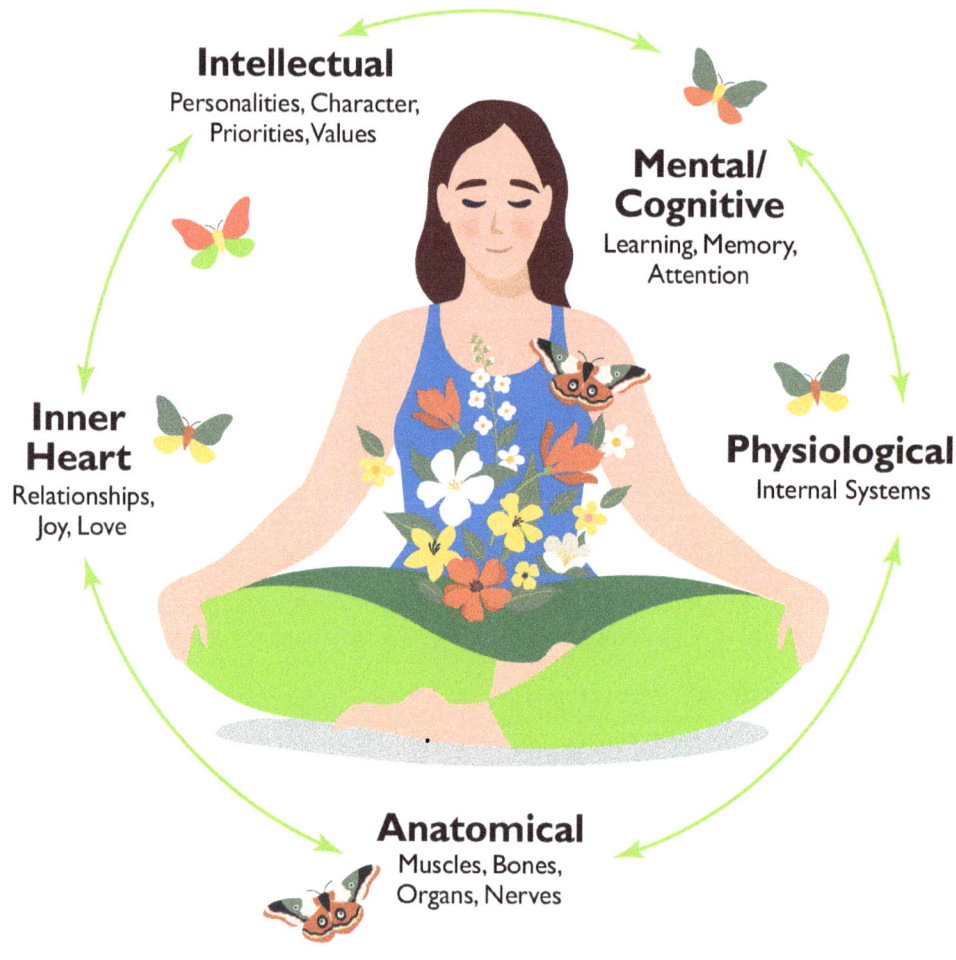

FIGURE 1. THE FIVE ASPECTS MODEL

attention. This attention helps us to observe objectively how we think, feel, and act. You can consider this as "being mindful." The result is an experience of being attuned to what we are doing right here and now. The deliberate, focused attention we use in yoga practice cultivates this kind of presence. In essence, we "sync up" the mind, body, and inner heart. When this happens, we generally feel a sense of balance, a feeling that things are in place.

My intention with this book is not to explain yoga fully. That tradition is far richer and more complex than I can hope to cover. Therefore, I've simplified my descriptions of yoga and its history in order to focus instead on its practical application to self-care. There are many resources that explain yoga more fully if you want to explore the topic further. You can see a short list under Resources at the end of the book.

## MY STORY

I was milling around a hallway at the Boston Sheraton, waiting to go into a class at a *Yoga Journal* conference. It was 2001. A soft-spoken woman and I began chatting. As women do, within a few minutes, we felt enough of a comfort level that she told me, "Yoga got me through breast cancer." She said she woke up and did her practice every day, no matter what. I didn't ask specific questions about her cancer or treatment. At my young age, I wasn't even sure what questions to ask. But I could picture her in the routine she described—on her yoga mat, early in the morning, still dark outside, the light from her TV flickering in her living room as she followed a yoga video.

Fast forward 18 years. Now that's me. Now I'm a person who can say, "yoga got me through breast cancer."

I already had an established yoga practice when I was diagnosed with invasive ductal carcinoma Stage 2a in August 2019. I had practiced yoga for over thirty years and was certified in yoga therapy, the clinical application of yoga to health conditions. Up to that point, I'd had excellent health, and I knew yoga could usually help me with whatever I needed

at a given time, along with any medical treatment I might need. But after the cancer diagnosis, my daily yoga practice became essential for calming my emotions, exercising my body, restoring my energy, and keeping my heart and soul moving in the right direction over eight months of treatment. I can't overstate how important regular practice was for me. It provided me with something I'd learned about from my yoga teacher: a "landing pad" for whatever state I found myself in when I awoke in the morning and a "launching pad" for heading toward my best possible state that day.

I was grateful for the training I'd had as a yoga therapist. Over the previous decade, I'd worked with many people, using the tools of yoga to help them manage the effects of their health conditions, like chronic pain, cardiovascular disease, autoimmune disorders, anxiety, depression, cancer, and more. I had also helped myself with yoga, from managing back pain to exploring my interpersonal relationships at a deep level. Yet, with all that experience, I was about to embark on an entirely new level of yoga therapy as I prepared to help myself through the most serious health challenge I had ever faced. Thankfully, I had a well-stocked toolkit of yoga practices.

The tradition of yoga therapy dates from the Vedic period, 1500–1100 BCE. The sages, or wise ones, of this tradition recognized that we are multidimensional beings—anatomical, physiological, cognitive, emotional, and spiritual—and our experiences affect us on all these levels. Despite this long-held understanding, the Western world is still working on how to treat the whole person. That integration of healthcare is what the field of yoga therapy is all about.

However, let me be clear: *competent, well-trained yoga therapists do not claim to treat cancer at a pathological level, nor do they think that is possible.* That's the domain of modern medicine. And it does a great job—evidence supports a 97 percent cure rate from the treatments I received. No amount of yoga is ever going to do that, and I wouldn't trade it for anything!

But what yoga therapy *can do,* and did for me, was help manage my symptoms, reduce my discomfort, increase my strength, bolster my confidence and courage, and most importantly, shed light on my relationship to this life I am living.

## I saw three categories of self-care I would need: *mental calm, physical strength, and spiritual connection.*

When I looked ahead to months of treatment, I decided to take time off from teaching yoga classes and seeing yoga therapy clients in order to take care of myself full time. I saw three categories of self-care I would need: *mental calm, physical strength, and spiritual connection.* The first thing I did was create a go-to practice which addressed all three categories. I used this practice to anchor and nourish me, day in and day out. There were days when I couldn't do the practice in its original form, or anywhere near its original form! For instance, it took ten days after my first round of chemo before I could return to any sort of practice. It felt so good to do a little movement after being stagnant and couch-bound. But when I got to the standing postures, like Warrior and Squat Pose, I suddenly felt short of breath. I'd never experienced that before. At first it made me feel anxious, which is a great way to bring on even more shortness of breath! I checked with my oncology nurse and learned that shortness of breath (aptly referred to as SOB, since that is what I muttered under my shortened breath!) was a common side effect of chemo. In fact, it was just one of many symptoms I would experience over the next few months. There was also nausea, fatigue, brain fog, constipation, hair loss, nail damage, sleep disruption, anxiety, and depression. Over months of treatment, I adapted my practice to meet each one of these situations.

Yoga philosophy says that we all have a light deep inside of us. We can think of that light as a metaphor representing our unchanging inner self, the part that is beyond the ever-changing outer world. This inner light fuels our natural ability to help ourselves, to care for ourselves. Sometimes our light becomes obscured by the ups and downs of life, like residue on a glass lamp cover. Think of yoga practice as a cloth that cleans the glass so your inner light can shine brightly again. Having cancer isn't the only time we should recognize our innate ability for self-care, but if an illness awakens that realization in us, then let's consider it a gift born of adversity.

Although many others will treat you and care for you as you go through cancer, please trust that you also have what it takes to help yourself, dear friend, through this experience and through your life.

**A QUICK NOTE ABOUT THE
"HOW YOGA HELPED" SECTIONS**

Following written instructions for a physical or mental exercise can feel disconnected at first, especially because a lot of these exercises start by telling you to close your eyes! Don't worry about that. Feel free to have the book right in front of you and look down at it as many times as you need to. Follow each step of the instructions in your own time. You can try this right now with the following simple exercise, which appears several times throughout the book:

# THREE SIMPLE BREATHS

1. Sit or lie down. When you are comfortable, take 3 simple breaths, slowly, in and out through your nose.

2. Let your breath take its time; there's no need to rush.

3. After 3 breaths, notice these things as best you can:

   - How does your body feel? Pause and really notice.

   - How does your breathing feel? Is it flowing smoothly? fast? slow? shallow? deep?

   - How does your mind feel? Consider a scale with *lethargic* at one end, *distracted* at the other end, and *calm and balanced* right in the middle. Where do you feel right now on that scale? There's no need to assume you're supposed to feel a certain way. Just pausing to notice your state of mind helps center you.

Hopefully, after these three simple breaths, you may feel more present (your five "aspects" may be more synced up), which is a great way to begin any exercise, conversation, or medical treatment.

## GUIDELINES FOR PRACTICING
## THE YOGA EXERCISES IN THIS BOOK

- Discuss with your healthcare provider how the gentle practices in this book may support your care plan.

- Listen to your body. Do not do any movement or exercise that causes pain. Modify any exercise to match your current condition.

- Never force the breath; always breathe smoothly and comfortably.

- Take several rounds of breath to gradually lengthen your breathing.

- Don't rush the breath or try to take deeper breaths than what feels natural.

- If you feel like an exercise is causing you to breathe faster or in a ragged manner, or if you feel light-headed, stop and let your breathing return to normal.

# CHAPTER 1

# I'LL BE FINE

In August 2019, I had just finished a session with a yoga therapy client when I saw my phone screen light up. I had been expecting a call from Dr. M. I knew what he was going to say even before I picked up the call because the radiologist who performed a biopsy on my left breast two days earlier had been pretty candid.

She'd said, "Even if this comes back benign, I'm going to recommend surgery. I don't like how it looks."

That, along with the fact that she also took tissue from one of my lymph nodes, painted a pretty clear picture. Still, at the time, my mind went to a safe haven of cautious optimism and practicality. *We won't know for sure until the results come back, so no use worrying now.*

Now, on the phone, Dr. M. confirmed it: cancer in the left breast that had spread to at least one lymph node. He had been my gynecologist for more than 25 years, had delivered both of my children, and was a teddy-bear of a guy. On the phone he was his usual encouraging self.

"The good news is we caught this early. And we know how to treat breast cancer so well these days. You're going to be just fine. Your first step is to get in touch with a surgeon."

The next several days were spent talking to family and friends and figuring out how to get started. I was surprised at how calm I was. I'm sure much of it came from not wanting to alarm my kids, who are, in fact, not kids but adults. The thought of their being scared of some unknown felt worse than the fear I had about the cancer. Maybe that sounds crazy, but that's motherhood. So, I acted like this was going to be fine, just like Dr. M. had said.

"I'm going to be fine. Think of all the people we know who've had breast cancer. They got it, they went through treatment, they're fine."

I must have said *fine* a million times that week.

*All shall be well and all shall be well and all manner of thing shall be well.*
ST. JULIAN OF NORWICH

On September 10, I was rolled on a gurney into an operating room at Memorial Sloan Kettering in New Jersey. The room was cold and extremely bright, humming with equipment. Gigantic lights, not yet turned on, hovered over the narrow table in the center of the room. A huge electronic screen filling most of one wall was lit up with all of my case information. Seeing my name up there, larger than life, made me laugh. *Next up, folks, it's Julie Shaw! She's here for a lumpectomy and sentinel node biopsy this morning. Let's give her a big hand!*

Despite my bright-side attitude, I could feel myself getting nervous and light-headed. This room was freaking intimidating. *Crap. I have cancer and these guys all realize that's serious shit, and I'm just getting the message. I may not be fine after all.* There were at least five people doing various things on pieces of equipment, their faces already hidden behind surgical masks. I thought I might possibly pass out (which was their objective anyway, but probably not like that), so I tried to stay engaged.

I chirped, "So, how's everyone feeling today?"

They seemed a little surprised (*you mean not every patient enquires about the surgical team's well-being?*), but quickly laughed and returned my greeting. One of them came over and said, "We're good to go. We've had our coffee. Our music is playing. All set. No worries."

A minute later I was unconscious.

Seventy-five minutes after that, I was waking up in a recovery room. My eyes wanted to stay closed. I wanted to sink back into sleep, but deep in my brain I knew the sooner I woke up, the sooner I could go home and get something to eat! With that motivation, I started doing an exercise I'd planned out before going into surgery. Inhaling slowly, I stretched open my right hand while flexing my left foot. Exhaling, I relaxed them. Then I did the opposite combination. I kept alternating back and forth, inhaling as I stretched and flexed, exhaling as I released.

We teach this kind of contralateral (right/left) and breath-centered movement in Viniyoga, the form of yoga I study. Viniyoga is known specifically for its careful attention to combining breath and movement. I remembered my teacher describing how he used this right/left hand and foot exercise when he was waking up from a surgery himself. It helped bring him out of a deep anesthesia fog. That story bolstered my confidence. I had embarked on a concerted effort to help take care of myself in all the ways I could, and this simple exercise was a first step.

The great news after the surgery was that only three lymph nodes needed to be removed in addition to the tumor in the left breast. I was so relieved, because I knew the more lymph nodes removed, the greater the chance of developing lymphedema, which could cause swelling in the arm. The swelling may be mild or quite severe, and it may not occur until months or years after cancer treatment. This is why you may see women who have had breast cancer wearing a compression sleeve—it's there to help keep lymph fluid flowing so the immune system can do its job. I really hoped my immune system would come out of this trauma with as little compromise as possible. I was counting on it to keep me healthy for many more years.

The fact that I received a lumpectomy rather than a mastectomy and extensive lymph node removal was the result of important ongoing research. I am so grateful to the researchers, physicians, nurses, technicians, and administrators who are doing that work, and especially to the women with breast cancer who took part in these studies. They took a chance on a newer procedure so that people like me could undergo a simpler surgery and easier recovery.

Two days after my surgery I was enjoying a live performance of *Wait, Wait, Don't Tell Me*, my favorite NPR show. It felt good to be out with my friend, Robyn, laughing and feeling normal. I knew recovering from the surgery was going to be the easiest part of this whole cancer treatment, so I planned to use this time to prepare my body and mind as best I could for the months of stronger treatment to come.

## HOW YOGA HELPED

On the next page is the exercise I used to help come out of the anesthesia fog after my surgery. It's a contralateral technique, engaging opposite sides of the body and brain. It's simple, but it takes focus, and builds focus the more you continue. You don't need to be coming out of surgery to use it; it's great any time you want to bring yourself out of a tired or distracted state. I was groggy in post-op, so it took determination to keep at it rather than falling back into that inviting deep sleep! I did the exercise for at least 15 minutes.

# LEFT/RIGHT FOCUSING EXERCISE

1. Begin in Position A. You can also do this exercise in a chair or on a bed.

POSITION A

2. Slowly stretch your **left hand** and flex your **right foot** at the same time (see Position B).

POSITION B

3. Then slowly relax them (see Position A).

4. Repeat with the opposite side, **right hand** and **left foot**.

5. Now match your breathing with the stretches: **inhale** as you stretch the hand and flex the foot; **exhale** slowly as you relax them.

6. **Continue alternating for several minutes** until you feel more alert.

Don't worry about how you look doing this exercise in the recovery room. If the nurses or technicians notice, just explain that you're doing an exercise to help yourself come out of the anesthesia. They'll be impressed at your initiative, and they may even ask you to teach it to them!

## HOW OTHERS CAN HELP

Have a loved one or friend who accompanies you to surgery read the exercise directions to you in the recovery room as you do the exercise.

# CHAPTER 2

# ARE YOU AFRAID I'LL DIE?

Embarking on cancer treatment, I knew there were big life lessons heading my way. One of the people who helped me navigate those lessons was my partner, Andy. I am profoundly grateful, over and over again, that he was there to help me through it. At the time I was diagnosed, he was working independently building a software app, so he had the flexibility to spend long stretches of time with me in New Jersey, returning to his home in Connecticut once a week to collect his mail and make sure his house was still standing.

Andy is a particular kind of caretaker. Recognizing a need and creating a way to fill it is one of his superpowers. As the primary parent after his divorce, he wanted to make sure his daughter experienced the presence of family, especially women. So, every Wednesday night for years running he held Prince Spaghetti Night, named for the 1970s TV commercial "Wednesday is Prince Spaghetti Night." He issued an open invitation to family and friends. Whoever showed up got "a plate of lousy spaghetti and salad from a bag," as he cheerfully tells it. Some nights there were five or six people, some nights as many as twenty. No one cared about the food (luckily!), but the conversation was lively, topical, and respectful. And his daughter was surrounded by caring people at her dinner table every week.

Years later, when Andy's mom, Catherine, was in poor health, barely getting out of bed and addicted to opioids prescribed unnecessarily by her doctor, Andy offered her a choice: "You can either go to a nursing home, where you'll probably die [the guy doesn't mince words!], or you can come live with me. But if you come to my place, you're getting off the drugs." Catherine chose what she would later call "Andy's Boot Camp." Over eight months, he weaned her off the pills, got her up and out of bed whether she liked it or not, and pretty much saved her life. She went on to live independently, free from the opioids, a much happier person for the final years of her 92-year-long life.

Andy applied his natural abilities for me when I got cancer. He observed what I needed and made it happen. One of his sweet and inspired suggestions was that my daughter Emma, 21 at the time, should come home from college for a weekend after my surgery and before I started chemotherapy. Andy and I talked about the idea in the large, airy lobby at Yale

University Hospital, where we were waiting for visiting hours to start on the maternity floor. Andy's daughter had just had a baby boy, Jack, the night before.

Andy said, "This seems like the perfect time for Emma to come home. If she visits now, she can see you looking strong. It could help her transition to the time when you'll be feeling lousy and your hair falls out."

When I called Emma to propose the idea, she began crying. The suggestion that she come home made her assume my situation was suddenly dire. I paced in a small circle, cell phone to one ear and a finger plugging the other to block out the noise of the busy hospital.

"That's not why I'm asking if you want to come home, honey. If things were that serious, I would tell you. I promise I'll always be honest with you."

That reassured her, but it wasn't the last tearful phone call we would share. A week or so after her visit, she called and again I could hear her crying.

"What is it?" I asked.

"I don't know."

"Are you worried about me?"

"Yes."

I could tell she couldn't put her fears into words. "Are you afraid I'm going to die?"

"Yes."

Now I could feel my own tears. Not so much from my fears, but because I hated knowing Emma was scared. Her young life was suddenly changed, and she couldn't unknow this reality. She had a couple friends who had lost their mothers to cancer. I knew at some point, later on, this trial would make her stronger, but right now things felt tender and tenuous and frightening.

"Honey, I know you're afraid of losing me, but that's not going to happen. At least not from this!" I forced a laugh. "It's not going to be easy, especially when I'm going through chemo. I'll probably look much worse than I really am. But it's an early-stage cancer and it's treatable."

I reminded her of my earlier promise. "I will always be honest with you. I'm not just saying these things to calm you down; I'm saying them because they are true."

I believed what I was saying to her. But I also sensed a familiar feeling I'd known from time to time as my kids were growing up—the feeling that *right now I'm telling you the truth, but the real truth is we never know what life will bring.* It's a dance between candor and reassurance. I guess between those two states lies hope.

*"Death is a challenge. It tells us not to waste time.*
*It tells us to say 'I love you' right now."*
LEO BUSCAGLIA

I was grateful for that call with Emma. It addressed what we'd left unsaid up to that point. Now I needed to have a version of this talk with my 25-year-old son, Michael. He probably had the same fears as Emma, but wouldn't bring them up because he wouldn't want to worry me. I decided to call him and start off with some concrete information about whatever was coming up next in my treatment. From there I told him about my conversation with Emma, as if it were another one of the things on my list to convey to him.

"I talked to Emma on the phone, and she was really upset. I asked if she was afraid that I might die from this and she said, 'yes.' So, I'm just letting you know the same thing I told her—that is not going to happen. I'm being straightforward with you guys, telling you everything I know. I just didn't want you to worry about that, okay?"

"Okay. Good to know."

A man of few words. Even though his style is quieter than Emma's, I knew he'd heard what I needed to say, and that he needed to hear it just as much as she had.

It felt like a weight had been lifted after these conversations with my kids. I believed now I could move forward being open and honest with them. When my mom was going through brain cancer twenty years before, I suspect there were things she kept from me. I understood then at some unspoken level, and I understood now at a much more conscious level, how complex it is to break frightening news to your children. I remember trying to figure out a way to tell Michael when he was six years old that his grandmother was dying. How do I even start such a conversation? In hindsight, I picked a stupid place and time, in the car after picking him up from a friend's house. My own anxiety and fear gave me a sense of urgency to get it over with, so I just blurted out, "You know Nana's been really sick, right? Well, the thing is her doctors are helping her all they can, but she probably isn't going to get better."

I'm sure I rambled on too long and made a simple truth sound very complicated. He was a little kid. He didn't know how to react or process something like that, so he just nodded. Over the next few weeks, I found ways to build the news into our everyday language, hopeful that it would become what it was— part of life. But I wish I'd done a better job with that particular conversation for Michael's sake. I wish I'd found ways to let us be sad out loud. Kids need their parents to model those experiences. If we keep things in, so do they. At least I'd figured that out by now, and as difficult as it was, I had to verbalize all the frightening stuff about the cancer so they could do the same.

Cancer, like any challenge, offers opportunities. It made me realize that someday I will want to be able to say good-bye to my children at the most simple and honest level. I won't want those words to go unsaid. Being able to get through the conversation about breast cancer now, as uncomfortable as it was, was one opportunity fulfilled. And it actually made communication about other things easier, as well. There's nothing like facing what we all know is inevitable to cure us of avoiding difficult conversations. For that, I am grateful to the cancer experience.

## HOW YOGA HELPED

During the time I was learning about my diagnosis and treatments, I had many moments of anxiety preparing to talk with my kids about all of it. When my mind started getting wound up, I would use a breathing technique to calm my nerves. I might do this several times a day.

Yoga offers a range of breathing techniques which can directly affect our autonomic (involuntary) nervous system. This is the part of our physiology that reacts to threatening situations. When we sense danger, this system turns on the fight/flight/ freeze response to prepare the body to protect itself, either by fighting, running away, or shifting into an immobilized physical and/or emotional state. When the threat is over, the relaxation response occurs and the body returns to a state of balance called homeostasis.

One of the most important things to understand about the fight/flight/freeze response is that it occurs not only when there is a real external threat, but also when we internally *imagine* a threat. Basically, that's worry or rumination or catastrophizing. The fight/

flight/freeze response is a life-saving adaptation when used periodically, as intended. But when we remain in that state because of persistent worry, our overall health suffers from the ongoing cascade of stress-fighting hormones coursing through our bloodstream which are not meant for daily functioning.

Here are two great breathing techniques for calming the nerves.

# RELAX WITH YOUR BREATH (SEE ALSO CHAPTERS 8, 9)

1. Lie on your stomach on the floor or on your bed (see Position A). Fold the arms, resting your head on your forearms. Position the arms so the base of your ribcage touches the floor, but the upper chest is away from the floor.

**POSITION A**

2. On **inhale**, feel your abdomen expand and press against the floor as your back rises.

3. On **exhale**, feel the abdomen relax as the back gently falls.

4. Keep your attention focused on the sensations of each breath. Let the body relax completely.

5. **Stay for 5–10 minutes,** then slowly sit up. Notice the ease of your breathing and your state of mind. (If it is not possible to lie on your stomach, lie on your back instead and place your hand on your belly. Feel the hand rise and fall with your breath.)

# CALMING LEFT INHALE/RIGHT EXHALE BREATH

(SEE ALSO CHAPTER 7)

It is not known how much biomedical understanding ancient yoga practitioners held, but their *prāṇāyāma* practices, or breath regulation, used highly effective techniques that we still use today to influence our body's functioning. The nasal passages have a direct connection, via nerve endings, to the brain. When we inhale through the left nostril, we stimulate inner structures associated with the relaxation side of our autonomic nervous system. Then, when we exhale through the right nostril, we sedate the structures associated with the fight/flight/freeze side of that system.[1] Several minutes of this exercise can have the effect of turning off fight/flight/freeze and turning on relaxation.

If you've practiced yoga before, you may be familiar with nostril breathing techniques. Often there is misunderstanding about how to block the nostrils. In many yoga classes, students are taught to block one nostril and leave the other open completely. That method misses a key step in how this technique works: The aim is to block one side completely, while creating a partial, or *"valved,"* opening at the other. The valve causes the air stream to become slower and stronger, lengthening the breath and increasing its effect on the nasal passages, and therefore on the autonomic nervous system.[2] It's not wrong to breathe through one fully open nostril and then the other—it's just a different technique than the one I use. I describe the practice below the way I learned it.

1. Sit tall (see Position A). Relax your shoulders and facial muscles and any other tension you may feel in your body. Start with **Three Simple Breaths** in and out through the nose.

POSITION A

2. Rest the thumb and ring finger of the right hand at the narrowest part of the nose, where the bone transitions to cartilage. You will be **partially blocking, or valving, both sides.** The circle in Figure 1 shows the spot where you place your thumb and finger on either side of the nose.

FIGURE 1: Start by placing thumb and ringer finger of right hand on either side of the nose at the spot indicated by the circle.

3. Now slide the thumb down to fully block the right nostril, and **inhale through the valved left side** (see Position B).

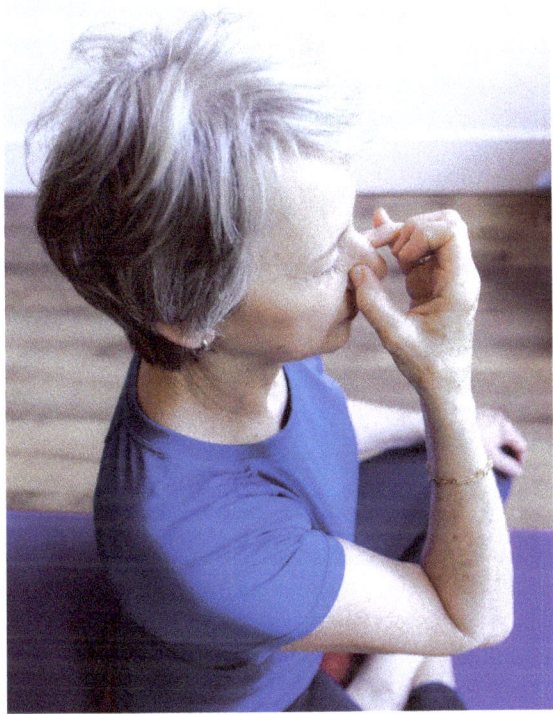

POSITION B

4. Then switch: Slide the ring finger down to fully block the left nostril, slide the thumb up to valve the right, and **exhale through the right** (see Position C).

POSITION C

5. Continue following the same pattern: **inhale left, exhale right.** Let your breath be slow and smooth.

6. Important note: *Going in the other direction, inhaling right, exhaling left, can be quite stimulating to the nervous system, and it is not recommended unless instructed by a skilled teacher for a specific purpose.*

7. Breathe slowly and smoothly. Gradually try to make your exhalations a little longer than your inhalations. Allow the pauses between breaths to occur naturally.

8. Start with a few rounds, working up to 2 minutes, and then 5 minutes or more. Once you get going, it becomes very relaxing, and you'll probably want to keep going.

If this particular valving technique is new to you, I encourage you to give it a try. You may find it creates a whole new experience with your breath practice!

## HOW OTHERS CAN HELP

Have a loved one or friend read the instructions to you a few times until you memorize the pattern. Or you could do the breath practice together. Having a partner, knowing someone is there with you, may help dissipate anxious feelings.

CHAPTER 3

# IT'S JUST PRACTICE

After my lumpectomy, there were several weeks of recovery before chemotherapy would start. I wanted to take advantage of the time to prepare my body and mind for the onslaught of drugs coming my way. Many friends and loved ones sent cards, texts, and gifts to encourage me. One gift was a blank journal with Van Gogh's *Starry Night* on the cover. I wasn't sure I would use it, even though I had kept other journals off and on for years. I admit, in the beginning, I felt allergic to the notion of writing down all my thoughts and feelings as I went through this "cancer journey." Weren't there already enough of those books? It seemed like there was a prescription for the experience in our culture, complete with a dress code, including anything pink, and a vocabulary that encouraged slogans like, "Be a Warrior, Not a Worrier!" In fact, someone said that to me when she learned I had cancer. She meant well, but it felt off-putting in a way, like a catchphrase from a coffee mug. Although I understood the enormous importance of breast cancer awareness in the public health arena, my instinct was to pull back from the media and the messaging. I needed to forge my own path.

Two days after my surgery, I woke early and tiptoed down the hall to the spare bedroom where I practiced yoga. I sat down to plan out the go-to practice that would start my day for many months to come. First, I needed a format. How was I going to approach this practice?

When I considered the strengths I would need for what lay ahead, it made me think of a particular Hindu goddess I had learned about. She is known as *Durgā*, and she represents these three attributes:

1. The **wisdom** to understand what is going on.
2. The **energy** to do what we must do.
3. The **blessings** to guide and protect us.

*Wisdom, energy, and blessings.* Those sounded like good qualities for guiding me through the multitude of appointments, decisions, side effects, and emotions that four months of chemotherapy and two months of radiation promised. I set to work sketching out my go-to practice on paper. It included several yoga tools to address symptoms at each layer in the Five Aspects Model: anatomical, physiological, mental/cognitive, intellectual, and heart-center.

## MY GO-TO PRACTICE

The practice I developed is quite detailed, because that was my personal preference. I knew I would need something that required a lot of focus to keep me anchored in the here and now rather than wandering off into worry. But another person might need a short and sweet practice. The key word is *personal*. A yoga practice should always be about the person doing it and the condition they are in at that time. My **go-to practice went as follows:**

### Personal Theme

I selected the theme of wisdom, energy, and blessings, as embodied by *Durgā* from the Hindu tradition. I also used a chant that represents these qualities: *Oṁ Aiṁ Hrīṁ Śhrīṁ Namaha*. The chant is in Sanskrit, the ancient language of yoga. The translation means, essentially, *I appreciate having the **wisdom**, **energy**, and **blessings** I need.*

*Oṁ* is an ancient mantra. A mantra is usually a sound, word, or phrase that helps transform our mindset when we repeat it systematically. The significance of *Oṁ* is profound in the yoga tradition, but very simply put, it is all that is, Absolute Reality. When used in a chant like the ones in this book, *Oṁ* is an invocation, a calling forth of that Absolute Reality as a starting point, or basis, for our intention.

### Opening

Yoga practice is like a journey—we travel from the external world to the internal and then back out again, hopefully changed for the better. My go-to practice began with a simple opening ritual at a small altar, which was just a wooden stool covered with a favorite blue scarf. Each item on the altar played a role (for more on these items, see Chapter 4).

First, I rang a tiny singing bowl. The vibrating sound called my attention to the fact that I was starting practice in the here and now with this ritual. It was an act of intention. I lit a candle to symbolize knowledge—through light we can "see" and "know."

I lit balsam-scented incense, and the burning stick turning to ash symbolized the transformation which is possible as I go through life. I sipped some water and tasted it, grateful for its wonder. I picked up a stone, like lavender quartz, and recognized the amazing fact that it came from somewhere on this earth and now I held it in my hand. These simple acts awakened the five senses.

We use our senses to take in information from the outside world and process it. In the case of a practice like this, it's a way to gather our typically externally-focused attention and purposely direct it inwards.

## Inner Focus

I closed my eyes and took time to notice how my body felt. I noticed the thoughts that came and went in my mind. I focused attention on following each breath in and out. After several moments, when I felt myself to be calm, alert, and present, I chanted my verse: *Oṁ Aiṁ Hriṁ Śhriṁ Namaha*.

Chanting adds important benefits to a yoga practice at many levels. At the physiological level, I felt the vibration from the chant lifting my energy. At the mental/cognitive level, by coordinating the chant with my movements, I kept my attention in the here and now. The chant also set the context for my practice, and I reflected on its meaning: *What is the wisdom I need today? What level of energy do I need and can I expect? What blessings surround and protect me as I wade into the unknown?* I tried to allow these reflections to surface with an open mind, resisting the temptation to answer or analyze anything.

## Movement

Then, I began a series of yoga postures. All of the postures were adapted to meet my body's needs that day. I warmed up the spine and major joints, then strengthened and balanced the lower back and hips, since that is where I am prone to discomfort under stress. I also included a couple of postures that stretched the chest and arms, which helped lift my energy and mood.

All of the postures were done in concert with the inhalation and exhalation. By linking the movement to our breath, we create a tangible connection between the body and the mind. In several postures, I also combined the chant with the movements. This specialized technique accomplishes several things: increases the intake of oxygen, which better meets the body's needs; enhances the beneficial effects of the yoga posture; vibrates the upper palate, which in turn vibrates an emotional center of the brain, and helps keep the mind focused on the intention of the practice.

Each time I chanted, I returned my attention to the qualities of *wisdom*, *energy*, and *blessings*. In the last pose, I lied down, giving my body and mind time to assimilate the effects of the practice so far.

## Breath Practice (Prāṇāyāma)

Sitting upright again, I reconnected to the sensation of my breath, as if it were flowing through a central channel in my body. I "felt" the inhalation flowing from the crown of my head to my heart (as my torso expanded), and the exhalation flowing from my heart to the crown (as I gently pulled the navel in). Once I firmly established this pattern, I silently repeated the chant with each inhalation and exhalation. I continued this for nine rounds of breath.

## Meditation

Everything to this point had been designed to prepare me for meditation. At that point, my body usually felt relaxed, my breath smooth and quiet, and my mind clear. I began meditating on the qualities of *Durga*.

I visualized myself entering what is known in the

yoga tradition as "the cave of the heart," my inner being. Everyone pictures this special place differently, and whatever image appears is the right one. I sometimes saw it as a soft and empty beach, other times as a quiet clearing in the woods with sunlight streaming down through tall trees.

I tuned into the physical and emotional effects of what I'd just done in my practice. Sometimes, I felt circulation or vibration from the movements. Other times, I felt a sense of peace after unplugging from the mind's ongoing chatter. I stayed inward and focused on the qualities of *wisdom*, *energy*, and *blessings* flowing into me from the sunlight. I recognized that I already possessed these qualities. I remembered my capacity for inner well-being and joy, despite my external condition that today. I sat in this state of meditation for as long as my mind remained calm and objective.

### Closing

When I sensed myself coming out of the meditative state, I recited the Durga chant three times (once silently, once softly, and once more loudly) to symbolize the return from the inner world to the outer. Then, I extinguished the candle on the altar and rang the singing bowl. I waited until the soft vibrating chime completely dissipated. I jotted a few reflections in my journal about how the practice went or what I learned. Writing often helped me face difficult emotions head on. And it also gave me the chance to chronicle all the joys I felt.

## HOW I USED MY GO-TO PRACTICE

For the next eight months, I used this practice as my template for cultivating the physical strength, mental calm, and spiritual connection which I knew at the outset was needed to go through cancer treatment. On some days, I needed to make the practice much shorter. I might do only the meditation and none of the postures. I might get down on the floor and do one simple movement in concert with the flow of my breath. Some days, I could only silently repeat the chant while lying on the sofa. No matter the details, the symbolism of Durgā became my guiding light, reminding me that I needed to keep moving forward.

On that first morning after I finished my go-to practice, I pulled out the Starry Night journal. I thought of the sweet friend who had given it to me. Sitting there in the still-quiet house, I got over whatever issues I had erected in my mind about the cliché of keeping a cancer journal, and just started writing. My first entry read:

*9/24/19 Durgā Practice*

*Ended with a deep relaxation and visualization: Thank you to lymph node that bore and contained the cancer for me. Thank you to two other nodes for being sacrificed. I'm grateful for their service and feel compassion for what went wrong with them. Visualizing the swelling going down, tissues repairing, remaining lymph nodes regrouping, skin healing, all returning to health and vitality.*

*Thank you, also, to Liz who made a beautiful prayer mala for me, and included rose quartz beads from her grandmother. I was so touched by that gift; reminds me of the positive energy being sent to me from so many people. How did I get so lucky?*

## THINKING ABOUT YOGA PRACTICE, RELIGION, AND SPIRITUALITY

One of the things I've loved most about studying yoga is the way it's helped me learn about different spiritual traditions. In all such traditions, people seek to connect to something greater than themselves, and they often do so through rituals like saying prayers, lighting candles, singing songs, moving their bodies, becoming quiet, even breathing.

Yoga is a system which can be applied to any spiritual tradition to help the practitioner connect to that which is highest for them. This connection is intended to happen at a physical, mental, and emotional level. This is why yoga is sometimes woven together with other belief systems, although yoga itself is not a religion. Studying yoga in the context of spirituality has helped me feel closer to something greater than me.

I'm not sure I can name it, but I like the description used by a wonderful teacher, Pandit Rajmani Tigunait: *ever-present, guiding intelligence.* [1]

Even though I grew up going to a Protestant church, as an adult I feel connected to a sense of spirit beyond that specific framework. I love sitting in front of my altar to start my yoga practice, just as I love entering the sanctity of a quiet church and then hearing the organ music swell. I love walking silently along a winding labyrinth or in a forest. I love feeling the vibration in my chest when I am chanting Vedic chants with my beloved yoga sangha, or "community." All of these experiences usher me into the presence of a spiritual essence which is beyond my ability to name.

## HOW YOGA HELPED

As you head into cancer treatment, or any other difficult experience, a personal practice can be a life raft to help you feel stable and strong. As you can tell from the description above, my go-to practice was quite detailed! But yours doesn't have to be.

You'll find a **sample go-to practice** in Chapter 22 which can be modified as needed. You can follow it as written, or just use a section or two. Maybe you just want to do the physical postures today. Or it might be a day for meditation and nothing else. It's your practice; own it and explore how it feels to take agency in your own health and well-being.

## HOW OTHERS CAN HELP

If you like having someone to exercise or do activities with, maybe you could enlist a yoga partner (or a couple of them!) to practice with you. They could even meet you online in a meeting platform like Zoom if you're not up for having people come over.

Or, if you don't have the energy to read through and experiment with this practice, or any others in the book, you could ask a friend or loved one to guide you through it. So often the people in our lives look for concrete ways to help us, and it can be taxing for you to find ways to let them help. Here is one way, all lined up for you to assign to a willing volunteer!

# CHAPTER 4

# ALTAR-ED REALITY

*Altar: A table or place serving as the center for a ritual*

MERRIAM-WEBSTER'S UNABRIDGED DICTIONARY

Before cancer, the "altar" for my yoga practice consisted of a candle, a singing bowl, and some incense. These were housed in the cabinet of my nightstand. I'd sit down cross-legged in the still-dark morning, open up the cabinet doors, and pull out my altar items. I'd ring the bowl, light the candle, then the incense, and get started. It took three decades of yoga practice to feel that even such a small, improvised altar made sense to me. I'm not saying it *should* take thirty years, that was just *my* timetable! Over those years, I gradually felt more comfortable with and connected to the various elements of yoga practice. The altar is one of those elements. It's like each person's "home base." It can be a place where we start and come back to each time we practice.

When I designed my go-to practice during cancer treatment, I expanded my altar. First of all, I brought the altar out of the cabinet. That was partly by necessity, since I moved my practice space from my bedroom to a spare room to avoid waking Andy so early in the mornings. But it was also partly by design. I

wanted to have a dedicated, "always open" practice space. All the items I gathered for this new altar came from precancer time, and meant something special to me. In many cases, the place where I got the item was the most important part.

I started out with a wooden stool and covered it with a blue scarf from a place called Ancient Yoga Center in Austin, Texas. I've spent a lot of time studying and teaching yoga there. I have so many sweet memories of walking the grounds with colleagues and friends, of the wonderful staff who hosted and fed us so well, and of the stunning peacocks that roam the grounds—males showing off and females making their funny calls that sound like *meow*. The blue scarf seemed like a good foundation for my new altar.

My singing bowl came from the gift shop at another yoga center where I've studied and taught, Mt. Madonna Center, in the mountains above Santa Cruz, California. It was the first of many items purchased at that gift shop. When I picked it out, I spent half an hour gently striking wooden mallets against singing bowls of various sizes, tilting my head toward the sound as if I had any idea what the different tones were all about! Eventually, I settled on the sweet, clear sound of the littlest one, which now sits on my altar.

The incense holder also came from Mt. Madonna Center. It's a tiny cast metal depiction of *Ganesh,* the Hindu deity who takes the form of an elephant. He's seen as a friend by many yogis (and non-yogis, for that matter). He is known as the "Remover of Obstacles," and represents intellect and wisdom.

In Viniyoga, we often start our training sessions with a chant about *Ganesh.* It took me a while to learn the Sanskrit words of the chant. Traditionally, students learn such chants by listening to the teacher, then repeating the exact pronunciation and intonation. I have a hard time learning words by sound, so I would garble the unfamiliar syllables and lag behind the teacher, faking my way through. (I'm sure a couple others were doing the same!) When I finally got a written copy of the chant, I memorized it quickly. Now the words and sounds flow off my tongue without trouble, and they link me directly to a sense of finding a way around any obstacle that might be in my way that day. Often, I realize the obstacle is my own perspective—*Ganesh* is a good cure for self-importance! (You can see a reference for the *Ganesh* chant in Resources at the end of the book.)

The candle holder on my altar was purchased when I attended a yoga workshop held at Mercy Center, a convent-turned-retreat center, in Burlingame, California. We stayed in the nuns' original rooms (they had all moved to a lovely assisted-living home just out back). I loved my room in the convent, with its tiny sink, desk, and closet. One day between sessions, I tiptoed into the convent chapel. There were ten or 12 rows of mahogany pews divided by a center aisle, facing a simple altar. Stained-glass windows lined the clerestory along the top of both side walls. Late afternoon sunlight streamed into the otherwise dark interior. I sat in a pew near the back. I was the only person there. I sat for 15 minutes, unmoving, eyes open, breathing, just being there. It was utterly silent. When I left, I noticed a stone plinth above the door carved with the verse: *I know the place where thy Glory dwells* (Psalms 26:8). I am not a student of the Bible, but something about those words stopped me in my tracks. My hand went to my heart. *Yes, with all certainty I know that whatever God is, that sacredness lives, dwells, in my own heart.*

On the last day of the retreat, I wandered into the gift shop (do you see a shopping theme here?), hoping to find a token with that verse on it. I didn't find one, but on my way out I spotted a votive candle holder with an inscription: *All shall be well and all shall be well and all manner of thing shall be well.* I pulled out my phone and Googled the verse. It was attributed to Julian of Norwich, a 14th century ascetic (another person with a similar name to mine!). She is noted as the author of the earliest surviving book in the English language written by a woman, *Revelations of Divine Love.* At the time of this retreat, I was going through a divorce and all the tumult that comes with it. This saint's message seemed like a pretty good one to take home with me. I'm glad to say eventually the struggles of divorce calmed down. Several years later, going through a bit more tumult in the form of breast cancer (and the COVID-19 pandemic), I was still comforted by those simple words.

Another item on my altar was a wooden carving of the symbol *Oṁ*. There is so much to study about *Oṁ*, and I will only touch on it in the broadest terms. *Oṁ* is an ancient *mantra*, which is usually a sound, word, or phrase that helps transform our mindset when we repeat it systematically. In this case, *Oṁ* is a living representation, in sound, of the Absolute Reality, all that is. Now that's *big*.

It has also become a ubiquitous symbol in the postmodern explosion of yoga's popularity, with a lot of people wearing and displaying it, perhaps without fully understanding its meaning. Therefore, I didn't want to take it lightly. After so many years of study, I had reached a point where I felt sure about what the symbol represented to me personally. I balanced the wooden carving on a tripod and set it on my altar. Seeing it there each day reminds me of something greater than just the here and now.

I draped two *malas,* or strands of meditation beads, over the *Oṁ* carving. One is from my dear, sweet friend, Alex, and includes three antique silver amulets from India, each depicting a different deity. One of those deities happens to be *Durgā,* the goddess I'd chosen for my cancer yoga practice, although Alex had no idea about that when she picked it out for me. The other *mala* was made for me by a student and friend named Liz (also my mom's name) who used rose quartz beads from a necklace that had been her grandmother's. Rose quartz is said to hold properties of healing and love, and I definitely feel those qualities when I hold that special strand of beads.

At the front of the altar, I placed a painting of pink, orange, and yellow morning light over a grassy field. It's one of many paintings by the chef at the Ancient Yoga Center in Austin (she is multitalented!). I later described the colors in this painting to my colleague, Ellen, which she wove into a visualization practice for me (see Chapter 5).

Finally, I placed a collection of stones on the altar, most from a shop called The Gem Stone Gallery in Frenchtown, New Jersey. My sister Grace had taken me there when I first got my cancer diagnosis. Both

Grace and the young woman who works there, Kelsey, made me feel really comfortable, even though I knew very little about stones and crystals. They encouraged me to walk around, pick up stones that appealed to me in some way, and just notice what I felt.

Now, dear Reader, I have to say that even though I am fully immersed in yoga practice, I'm still *me,* which is to say, I'm pretty linear and cerebral! For that reason, it took me a few trips to the gem store to loosen up and get out of my head. Along the way, I found myself doing just what Grace and Kelsey suggested—picking up stones. And then waiting. Maybe I'd put a couple back and walk away. Whatever I ended up with in my hands after half an hour or so was what came home with me.

My collection grew to include lavender quartz, ruby fuchsite, bumble bee jasper, morganite, selenite, jade, citrine, amethyst, and so many more. At first, I studied the little cards that came with each stone, trying to memorize their supposed properties (my cerebral side at it again!). Quartz is associated with love; selenite stimulates brain activity. I didn't understand how those properties were determined, but I did know that every piece of matter vibrates. So, I stopped *thinking* about the stones and began to enjoy the look and feel of them. Now, I may pick up one to hold during meditation, and I don't think about why I'm selecting that particular one. I can't explain it, but to me these stones give off "good vibes."

Pulling together the items on my altar helped me create an "always-open" practice space. It kept me in a positive mindset of healing awareness throughout the days of chemotherapy and radiation. Each piece on the altar held significance, representing many points along the way in my life. But I honestly hadn't been ready to create an altar until now. Not because I suddenly "got religion" after finding out I had cancer. But because I understood that even though each item on the altar holds meaning, the items themselves are placeholders for the essence they represent—simply, and complexly, the mystery of life.

## HOW YOGA HELPED

### Setting up a Practice Space

Some of the tips and techniques in this book can be done anywhere—in the waiting room at a doctor's office, lying on the sofa, or sitting at a desk. But some require a more dedicated space. I encourage you to set up your own place where you can go to reconnect with your sources of inspiration and strength. Here are a few ideas:

**Carve out space.** Select a spot that can either remain set up or can be easily converted into a practice space each day. Space can be at a premium for many people, so you may need to be creative and flexible. Ideally, it will be a quiet spot. Being near a window is always a plus. I love to start my practice before sunrise and see the light dawning over time.

**Roll out your mat—or not.** Technically, you don't need a yoga mat to practice yoga. You just need you. But it helps to have a floor covering where you can lie down comfortably and do yoga postures without slipping, and it turns out a yoga mat works really well for that! Mats are available widely, but I recommend purchasing from a yoga supply source, rather than a big box store or supermarket. That's because some of the cheaper brands are actually slippery, which is the opposite of what you want. (See Resources at the end of the book for suggestions.) You may also choose to do your yoga practice on a chair, or on your bed. Don't let the fact that you can't get down on the floor make you think you can't do yoga! And where you do your practice may well change over time.

**Add extras—or not.** Some people may want nothing more than a mat placed in front of a window—the

perfect minimalist practice space. Others may want to include a collection of items that uplift and nurture them. Whether you prefer the term *altar* or *centerpiece* or *home base,* what's important is that these special objects have authentic meaning *for you,* that they remind you of inner sources of inspiration, and therefore foster your self-caring ritual. When you place something on your home base, be clear about why you're putting it there. For example: *This stone from Zion National Park makes me think of the astounding beauty of this earth.* Or: *This photo of a tiny chapel I saw tucked into a remote hillside reminds me of how faith finds its way to everywhere.*

**Bring your inspirational items into your practice.** Maybe just having your items collected on a table suits you best. Or maybe you'd like to bring these items in your practice (see the box below). Just be sure it feels sincere to you.

## BRINGING RITUAL INTO YOUR PRACTICE

Consider any or all of these ways of bringing ritual into your practice, or create your own:

- Ring a chime or singing bowl to call your attention and remind yourself that you are starting an intentional practice.

- Light a candle to awaken your ability to learn and know at a cognitive level as well as at a deeper, inner level.

- Light incense to symbolize transformation (for instance, the yoga practice may transform neck stiffness into relaxation, and a worried mind into a calmer, more peaceful state).

- Read a poem or say a prayer or an intention to reinforce the reason for practice.

- Do yoga postures and breath exercises to enhance physical energy.

- Meditate holding prayer beads to count each breath or mantra (chant) to focus the mind and usher in a state of inner stillness.

- Extinguish the candle, ring the chime to close the practice.

## HOW OTHERS CAN HELP

If you'd like to set up a practice space and an altar but aren't feeling up to it, ask for help. Maybe there's someone in your life who practices yoga or has a strong connection to spirituality who would love to help with something important and meaningful to you like creating a special practice area for you.

# CHAPTER 5

# I'M POSITIVE

One of the gifts I received soon after being diagnosed with cancer was a coloring book titled, *F*#! Breast Cancer.* Although I was grateful for the encouragement behind the gift, I wasn't crazy about the message. I knew cancer cells were just my own cells which had turned from good to bad. I didn't like the idea of hating my own cells, setting up an enemy relationship with tissues that had undergone some sad conversion.

I wanted to keep things as positive as possible, down to the words I was using and the thoughts I was thinking. The fact that this was a conscious act is what kept it from feeling like I was trying to talk myself into believing everything would be okay. Instead, I was making a deliberate decision to use positivity as a tool for my health.

A few years earlier, I had worked on an integrative health team delivering a lifestyle change program, developed by Dr. Dean Ornish, to cardiac patients.[1] My role was to teach the participants how to use yoga techniques to reduce their stress levels. One of the key techniques we taught was positive imagery. This was the trickiest part of my job. Most of the people in the program had never practiced yoga before, but they could understand simple postures, breath work, and guided relaxation because they could feel the immediate results of those techniques. Selling them on the value of positive imagery was much harder. Even though we provided clinical research to support it, many of them just couldn't buy into "imagining" themselves to health.

Now that I was a patient myself, positive imagery quickly became one of the most important tools I had. Positive imagery and visualization are correlated with improved health and longer life.[2][3][4] Psychologists and neuroscientists who study neuroplasticity, the brain's ability to change, have shown that repeated patterns of mental activity actually change the brain's structure and function. The phrase "neurons that fire together wire together" is often used to describe this phenomenon. In other words, *you become what you think*. Neuroscientist Richard Davidson's research showed that meditation can alter patterns of activity in the brain to strengthen optimism and a sense of well-being.[5] Bottom line: If you consciously practice a positive mindset, your brain changes to reflect that positivity, which can affect the rest of your body and your health. Conversely, a negative mindset creates negative effects.[6]

*"The moment you change your perception is the moment you rewrite the chemistry of your body."*
**BRUCE H. LIPTON, PH.D.**

I also learned about the mind and its ability to change by studying a foundational yoga text: *The Yoga Sutra of Patañjali.* Dated to approximately 400 CE and attributed to a sage known as *Patañjali,* the *Yoga Sutra* outlines what yoga is and how to practice it. It starts out by saying, in essence:

*Yoga is the ability to direct and focus mental activity.*

*With that focused mind, we gain the ability to see what is most profound and important within us.*

*Otherwise, when the mind wanders aimlessly, we identify ourselves with those aimless wanderings.*[7]

Even 2,000 years ago, *Patañjali* understood the notion of "you become what you think." He is saying your inner self is something much deeper than your busy mind. Importantly, *until we understand this idea*, we continue to mistake our busy minds for our inner being. As long as we continue to do that, we miss out on a fundamental opportunity for the true happiness and well-being that comes from abiding in our true nature. Whether through the lens of modern neuropsychology or ancient yoga, the message is the same—the conscious choices we make about our mindset matters.

Even without the scientific evidence or yogic teachings, it's always been my nature to be positive. My maternal grandmother, Nana Weinsheimer, especially influenced me this way. Nana was a kind, resourceful, no-nonsense person who generally made the best of things. That doesn't mean she didn't have difficulty or pain in her life. But she persevered. She went to college in 1922 and worked as a teacher for more than thirty years. She was a young woman during the Depression. She cared for her husband when he was diagnosed at age 42 with Parkinson's disease until his death at 76. She cared for her two children, her live-in father-in-law, and later, my sister and me. She lived the last 14 years of her life in a nursing home, far longer than the average time most people survive in those settings. Every day in the nursing home, she got up and got dressed, even though she used a wheelchair by that time. At 93, she survived the death of her youngest daughter, my mom. Nana showed me something I would learn in a more formal way years later through the lens of yoga—we can't always control our situation, but we can control how we respond to it and what we learn from it. She never specifically articulated that lesson; she just demonstrated it by being who she was. She lived to be 99. I have to believe her mindset had something to do with that.

Before embarking on four months of chemo, I made a conscious decision to include positive imagery in my yoga practice. I turned to a friend and colleague, Ellen, to help me create a positive imagery practice. Ellen was a social worker and yoga thera-pist who helped others deal with cancer and end of life. She herself was a cancer survivor for many years until her passing in 2021. As we talked, she drew from our conversation the images and concepts that were important to me at the start of the chemo treatment process. I described a vision I'd had of all the people in my life—family, friends old and new, colleagues from every job I'd ever had, and even my entire high school marching band!—congregating around me for a sort of "support picnic." I had also been visualizing the pastel colors from the painting at my yoga altar. I saw yellow, orange, and rose infusing the cells of my body with healing light. And I told Ellen I was using the goddess *Durgā,* the embodiment of wisdom, energy, and blessings, as my primary guiding inten-tion in every yoga practice.

At our next appointment, Ellen led me through a visualization (which she recorded for future use) that included all of my images. She wove them together skillfully and simply, offering back my own "healing medicine." One of my favorite parts came near the end. She said, "Let your awareness settle into this pastel-filled heart, allowing and inviting your *sangha* [a Sanskrit word for *community*], your ancestors and angels to visit, to be with you, to *accompany* you, in whatever way is just right for you."

One of the things that serious illness can do is erode our endurance, our motivation to keep doing the things that help us stay strong. It becomes an effort to keep a positive mindset. So having a tool like this meditation, consistently reminding me to *choose* pos-itive thinking, was invaluable. I used it many times before chemotherapy started. It prepared me for stay-ing the course through those rough four months.

This practice raised powerful emotions about the nature of existence. I purposely chose images that induced such deep emotions because I wanted to go beyond my fears about mortality. I wanted to con-nect with the ineffable spirit I believed existed within me, one that transcended the inevitable changes and circumstances I anticipated going through. I felt this was a now-or-never opportunity to face my fears and, I hoped, come through even stronger. This meditation helped me access an experience of inner joy despite my outer circumstances.

That said, I admit I used this imagery practice to bolster that positive trend when I was feeling strong to begin with. I used it when I had the physical and emotional reserves to face the poignancy the practice itself surfaced. On really hard days, though, when I felt less stable, I turned to much simpler tools for shifting my mindset from a negative state to at least neutral. The key was to keep taking steps, no matter how small, toward the positive side.

## HOW YOGA HELPED

We hear a lot about "the power of positive thinking." Yoga offers a way to put that adage into action. Below, and on the following pages, you'll find three options for shifting your mindset toward a positive and beneficial outlook.

### Sample Positive Imagery Script

If this sample script appeals to you, feel free to use it for yourself. You might also want to record yourself or a friend reading the script.

*Instructions to the script reader:*

- Read slowly and thoughtfully in your normal voice; the practice below will take 20–30 minutes.

- Instructions ***in italics*** are directions to the reader and are not to be read aloud.

# POSITIVE IMAGERY SCRIPT

1. Please lie down. Get comfortable. Cover up to stay warm if you like. *(Pause; allow time for listener to get settled.)*

2. Take a few long, smooth breaths. Let your whole body relax. *(Pause; allow time for listener to relax.)*

3. Continue to breathe slowly and smoothly as we do a relaxation exercise. *(Pause between each instruction below.)*

4. Bring your attention to your right foot.

5. Inhale and flex the ankle. Hold it. Feel the tension.

6. Exhale and relax the foot.

7. Bring your attention to your right leg.

8. Inhale and tighten all the muscles of the leg. Hold it. Feel the tension.

9. Exhale and relax the leg.

   *(Continue, slowly, in the same manner; progressing as follows: left foot; left leg; buttocks; right hand; right arm; left hand; left arm; shoulders; facial muscles.)*

10. Bring to mind an image, a place, or an idea that is nourishing to you. Picture it in as much detail as possible, noticing color, textures, smells, sounds, light, and sensations.

11. Focus on how your nourishing image is benefitting you. Take time to immerse yourself in this imagery.

    *(Pause to allow time for visualizing and focusing.)*

12. Tune into how your body feels as you visualize your nourishing image. Immerse yourself in that feeling.

    *(Pause to allow time for feeling.)*

13. Recognize that you have the capacity to create a positive mental state as you go through treatments. Recall that a positive mindset has a positive impact on the brain and on well-being. Rest in that knowledge.

    *(Pause to allow time for resting.)*

14. Prepare to emerge from your relaxation. Slowly deepen your breath. Feel vital energy returning to your limbs, to your lungs and heart, to your brain. Keep your focus inward and gently rotate your wrists and ankles. Roll to your side and carefully push yourself to sitting. Gently open your eyes to conclude your practice.

15. You may want to jot a few notes in a journal to reflect on your experience.

## CREATE YOUR OWN SCRIPT

If you prefer, you can create your own positive imagery script. Choose images or themes that nourish, uplift, and strengthen you. They could be mental pictures, colors, scents, sensations, places, ideas, anything that comes naturally to mind. Different people will use different approaches. For example:

- Images that directly affect the illness, like Ms. Pac-Man gobbling up cancer cells or a superhero zapping each cell with a direct hit.

- Images that induce a feeling of comfort and well-being, like a cherished place or a calming presence.

- Images that recall an accomplishment of yours which required confidence and strength, like going on a job interview, delivering a speech, or competing in a triathlon. Your images may even change over time. It only matters that the contents of your practice feel real to you.

Once you've selected your images, start with a relaxation exercise like the one outlined in the prior example. A relaxed body leads to a relaxed mind, which can hold a visualization much longer than a busy mind.

Then, weave your uplifting images into the script. Keep it simple, with short, clear sentences. Maybe in your script you'll simply visualize or access each image in turn, seeing, touching, hearing, even smelling it. The more senses we use, the more effective the power of positive thinking will be. Or maybe you'll pull the ideas together into a "story" that takes you on a little journey.

The way this practice works is by holding your attention on the imagery, so take time to allow the importance of each idea to sink in and provide you with support and nourishment. Think of your images as "self-medicine," and give yourself a healthy dose. The more often, the better.

## SIMPLER YOGA TOOLS FOR SHIFTING MINDSET

Sometimes, I was too emotionally fragile to dive deeply into my imagery practice because it brought up strong, existential themes. If I didn't feel ready to take on those deep thoughts, I turned to these simpler tools:

- "Left/Right Focusing Exercise" (see Chapter 1)
- "Left Inhale/Right Exhale" (see Chapter 2)
- "Relax with Your Breath" (see Chapter 2)

## HOW OTHERS CAN HELP

This is a perfect opportunity for a friend or loved one to help. Let them read the sample script I've provided, or help you write out your own. Then they can lead you through it, or make a recording of the instructions so you can use it whenever you want to.

# CHAPTER 6

# LET'S GET THE CHEMO SHOW ON THE ROAD

Day one of chemotherapy was October 3, 2019. I rose early and did my yoga practice, connecting to the qualities of *wisdom, energy, and blessings* to bolster me. I felt healthy and ready to get things underway. I was so fortunate that Memorial Sloan-Kettering had a treatment facility ten minutes from my home in suburban New Jersey. Day one established the routine that Andy and I would follow every other Thursday for the next four months. First, I went to the lab. They drew blood to make sure my white blood cell count was high enough to get treatment that day. Luckily, in the four months of chemo, I never had to postpone a treatment because of a low white cell count.

Next, we saw my oncologist, Dr. A. She was in her forties or fifties with thick, wavy hair and always wore a wrist full of silver bracelets that jangled pleasantly. My first meeting with her, right after my diagnosis several weeks earlier, had been a bit daunting. She ran through a ton of medical information and barely let me get a word in. Even Andy, who can usually

sum up a research article with no problem, admitted after the appointment that he hadn't caught everything she said!

I knew Dr. A. was a respected researcher and clinician, and I wanted her expertise. I thought about what I needed to do to get comfortable with her. By the time I'd seen her a few times, I learned to pare down my questions to the essentials, focusing on what I needed to know on that day. That worked well. In chatting we discovered we both had daughters in college in Indiana. She surprised me by ending every appointment with a big hug. That connection was part of her style too, and it felt genuine. In the midst of a huge cancer hospital system, this doctor didn't shy away from the medicine of human touch.

The lesson for me was that despite my initial discomfort with Dr. A's communication style, she wasn't necessarily the one who needed to change. I saw that many of my questions were actually just manifestations of the natural anxiety that comes up when you're going through something big or new, like cancer treatment. When I focused on the questions that she was expert at (Which of the three antinausea meds you've prescribed should I try first?) and let go of those that I was more likely to find answers for elsewhere (What's the correlation between the herb valerian and estrogen?), many of the anxieties dissipated.

Next, Andy and I moved on to the chemo suite waiting room. I dug into a classic New Jersey egg and cheese sandwich that we'd bought on the way to the appointment. The steroids I took before every treatment gave me a huge appetite. And for the time being, all thoughts of a health-food-only diet were off. I was *hungry* and could use a few pounds, so I ate what my body craved. (This particular approach may not be for everyone, and I wondered now and then if I'd skipped some of my cravings, like the occasional burger, would I have felt a little better? Honestly, in my case, I really don't think it would have made a big difference. Even when I ate the best things possible, I still felt like crap!)

Soon my sister Grace arrived. She came to every one of my eight chemo appointments, working around her busy schedule as a university professor. My sister is a quiet person, extremely intelligent, thoughtful, and empathetic. On the day I got the news of my breast cancer, she drove to my house. It was a sunny August day. We sat on my screened porch. The ceiling fan circled noiselessly overhead. Grace swayed back and forth in a rocker as she listened to all the information I had. Eighteen months older than me, she'd had precancer breast health issues, and saw an oncologist annually. She asked calm and measured questions and offered input based on her own experiences, which helped me stay calm myself.

"I can put you in touch with my oncologist. She is truly the best doctor I've ever seen. She takes so much time and really explains the big picture."

When I ultimately decided to go to Sloan-Kettering instead of Grace's doctor, she understood and supported me. "The most important thing is to find the place that's right for you."

I knew my having cancer was probably frightening for Grace. But she didn't bring that up. Instead, she hugged me tightly, which was somewhat unusual for us even though we are quite close, and said, "Whatever you need, Sis, I'm here for you." Maybe having to face right up to the fact of cancer let a little steam out of its threat. Here it was, the scary thing that seemed to loom for so many people, and we were going to go through it together. (As it turned out, four years after this conversation, my sister made the decision to have a prophylactic bilateral mastectomy after years of precancerous biopsies. After the procedure, she said she finally felt free!)

My other indispensable partner for this experience was Andy. Somehow the internet dating stars had lined up on one particular day when we both signed up for the same free messaging weekend on the dating app MeetMindful. I was drawn to it because I had hoped to meet someone who really was mindful, who had taken a look at his life so far and recognized his own behavior. (Anyone who has done online date is now laughing hysterically. But, in fact, I did find that person!) Andy was drawn to it because it was free. We met for a walk in March 2016 and have been together ever since.

One thing that drew me to Andy was his optimism. He credits his outlook on life to an early childhood case of strep which attacked his kidney and became life-threatening. I remember our first date, walking through the woods, when he told me matter-of-factly, "I was in the hospital for over a year, and it was really a dire situation, but I still felt the joy of life [*yes, he really says those things!*]. I knew the people taking care of me loved me—the nurses were so nice! Even though I was just a little kid, somehow I learned that life could be short but still hold beauty. I guess I've carried that with me since then."

Indeed, without fail, Andy greets every day as if it is the most beautiful so far in history. "What a *spectacular* morning!" Before every meal, even when I plop a tuna fish sandwich in front of him, he says, "Thank you for the bounty, honey!" After the first sip of morning coffee, he closes his eyes and says, "Mmm, the elixir of life." He's predictable in a way that nourishes the soul, never giving up on life's possibilities. What a blessing it is to have a partner fully committed to the bright side, but not afraid to look at reality. "Oh, you're going to feel really raw for a few days after chemo, honey." Andy doesn't sugarcoat things, he doesn't know how. I loved the freedom that gave me not to have to choose my words carefully with him. We could both handle whatever needed to be said.

When I was halfway through my egg sandwich and had sent Andy to the snack bar for something chocolate, a nurse came to escort us to our chemo "pod." I was happy to see it had a large window with a view of the woods. My nurse, and all the other staff, were kind and considerate and calmly professional. It took the nurse about half an hour to set up my IV

and start the pretreatment drugs designed to prevent my system from revolting against the actual chemotherapy drugs. When it was time for the chemo treatment, she donned a gown and gloves, since the drugs are so toxic. *Yikes. Not very reassuring.* Another nurse, also in a gown and gloves, joined her and together they checked and double-checked the label on the chemo packaging and the ID band on my wrist. Then my nurse hung a bag filled with a thick, cream-colored liquid on my IV pole, which, I admit, made me really queasy even looking at it. It was anastrozole/cyclophosphamide, or A/C, the drug combination I would receive for my first four treatments. The nurse sat down next to me and said she would be "pushing" the drugs manually through my IV in order to monitor my reaction. If I felt any discomfort, like a sudden headache or dizziness or heat, I was supposed to tell her immediately.

I laughed, which seemed like the best reaction to have at that moment, and said, "Okay. Let 'er rip!"

I guess it's no surprise that chemo treatment is a multilayered emotional experience. There were several things going on in my head at the same time. At one level, I could see and hear myself acting like my paternal grandmother, Nana Mest. She was quiet, docile. Everything was always "just fine." I'd seen her in an emergency room wearing the same smile she had when we went out for ice cream. I didn't know what was going on inside her head, and she may not have understood the medical treatments that were happening, but her coping mechanism of agreeableness seemed to work for her—she lived to be 95.

It was about believing that whatever happened,
we would get through it one way or another.

Additionally, I had the prevailing attitude that "things will be okay" from my mom. This despite the fact that she suffered from depression throughout her life. I can still feel my mom's arms around me and hear her saying, "Things will work out." It didn't matter what the problem was or how old I was. I simply believed her. It wasn't about blind idealism or refusing to believe that anything bad could happen. It was about believing that whatever happened, we would get through it one way or another.

Finally, I had the knowledge and experience I'd gained from years of studying and practicing yoga, along with reading about other contemplative and spiritual traditions. These provided me with a framework for considering my inner life. I was firmly established in the belief that my inner self was whole and unchanging, despite external conditions.

All of these reactions were happening simultaneously. And they seemed to be helping me stay calm and grounded in my reclining chemo chair. I didn't like the idea of some impending pain caused by a toxic drug being slowly pushed into my veins. But I kept it clear in my mind that this moment was not the whole thing, it was just what I needed to deal with right now. I was very conscious at every chemo trip not to wander into "what if's," nor did I drop into symbolic imagery, seeing the equipment and the staff in their royal blue uniforms as representing my fate, my mortality. I stayed away from that. Sometimes I did it by nodding and smiling like Nana Mest, and sometimes I did it by silently repeating the *mantra* from my yoga practice, calling forth wisdom, energy, and blessings. Both approaches worked. And the beautiful part is, it wasn't hard to do. Whatever had happened in my life so far had prepared me to be calm, and I was.

As the nurse held my right arm with one hand and "pushed" the A/C slowly through an auxiliary syringe with the other, I closed my eyes and focused on my breathing. Slow breath in, slow breath out. Occasionally the nurse would ask, "Are you still with me?" and I would smile and nod "yes." But inwardly I was repeating my *mantra*: *Oṁ Aiṁ Hriṁ Śhriṁ Namaha—I have the wisdom, energy, and blessings I need in this moment. And now, in this moment. And in this one.*

Just before the last of the A/C had drained from the bag, I felt a sudden, slight pressure in my sinuses. *Oh. Okay. That wasn't too bad.* I told the nurse and she slowed down the drip. Almost immediately the pressure subsided. I was close to the end of my first round of chemo. It had taken about an hour and a half. I checked in with my body—what was I feeling? A little tender at the IV site, cold from the fluids, maybe a little tired.

But mostly, *hungry*.

## HOW YOGA HELPED

During an experience like chemotherapy, we might feel nervous, jumpy, or scared. Where the mind goes, the body follows, and an anxious mind can lead to increased blood pressure, heart rate, respiration, insulin production, and a number of other negative health responses. Luckily, the reverse is true—a calm mind can reverse those physical settings. Here's where a good coping mechanism comes in handy. I'm not suggesting we engage in denial about chemotherapy, but rather find a healthy focusing strategy to help keep our minds and bodies in as calm a state as possible, so the process can go smoothly and the medicine can do its job optimally.

Below are a few focusing tools to try while you are in the chemo chair. If you find yourself drifting into what-if scenarios (*What if I have an allergic reaction? What if I get nauseous immediately?*), try redirecting your attention back to the exercise. If that doesn't work, try another strategy. Often, a combination of strategies will work best. And remember, this is not about perfection; it's about making it through the couple hours in the chemo suite in a relatively calm state. That's all you need to do.

### *Focusing on External Things*

*Engage in Conversation.* Talk with family, friends, medical staff. Pick a topic that engages you while allowing you to remain calm. For some, this may be discussing a hobby. For others, it may be discussing the latest research on the treatment you're receiving, or the nuts and bolts of how the nurse is administering your medicine. Some of us do better with some distance between us and the procedure, while others thrive on knowing all they can about every step. The best choice is the one that helps you feel calm in that chair without shifting into a denial state.

*Watch the World Go By.* If you're lucky enough to be near a window as I was during my chemo sessions, you can use the outdoors as your focusing tool. Watch the clouds morph into new shapes or the trees sway in the wind. See birds fly, people come and go, traffic stream by. Remember the intention is to stay present. If you find yourself drifting into, *I wish I was out there, driving around like those people, without a care in the world,* then select a different strategy. Better yet, try a classic yoga tip: Reframe the situation. Remember that many of the people in those cars are also dealing with difficulty, just like you. You may recognize a sense of human connection as we all do our best in our own current circumstances.

*Listen to Music, Podcasts, Audio Books.* Choose content that engages you in a relaxed way. Sometimes this means taking a look at your information-consuming habits. Notice if listening to politics or crime podcasts, for instance, actually soothes you or stirs an agitation you've gotten used to. This is a time to really *notice* your physical, mental, and emotional states and how you react to things. I imagine the body receives and utilizes the chemotherapy more easily and effectively if we foster a serene mindset.

*Hand or Shoulder Massage.* Often those accompanying you to chemo will want to help in a tangible way. A hand or shoulder massage (on your nontreatment side) can be a perfect gift. It employs the warmth of human touch, along with the release of tension. Put all of your attention into the physical experience of the massage—don't just let it fill time without *feeling* it! Simple massage like this doesn't require any special training, just human touch.

## Focusing on Internal Things

These exercises worked especially well for me during moments of anxiety. For example, I used an internal focus every time a nurse was inserting my IV, which always took multiple attempts at various spots on my arm and hand. Without fail, every nurse I had would see my eyes closed and hear my slow, purposeful breathing and ask, "Are you still with me?" I would keep my eyes closed and say, "I'm in my happy place."

*Hand Exercises with Breath and Movement.* These exercises engage both sides of the brain, which is excellent for sustaining focus. Coordinating movement with the breath creates a real-time connection between body and mind, as well as slowing down breath rate, blood pressure, and heart rate. Start with both hands in loose fists. Be gentle with the hand on the IV side—no tight fist or excess movement. Try any of the versions below, repeating for several rounds.

- As you slowly inhale, open all the fingers. As you slowly exhale, close all the fingers.

- On inhale, open the fingers one at a time. On exhale, close the fingers one at a time.

- You could play with the order in which you open/close the fingers; for example, open thumb-to-pinkie and close in the same order. Or close the fingers in the opposite order.

- Try doing the above alternating right and left hands. There are many ways to vary this theme; the more patterns you employ, the more focus is required. Explore your own dexterity and creativity.

*Follow Your Breath.* This gentle, cyclical practice is a simple form of meditation. Settle into a smooth rhythm of breathing. Relax your facial muscles, shoulders, arms, hands, and so on down the body. As you try one of the following versions of the exercise, if your mind wanders, just bring it back and pick up where you left off. It doesn't matter how many times you start over; the important part is staying committed to bringing your attention back to the exercise. Here are a few options:

- Count internally, saying "one" on inhalation and "two" on exhalation. Continue up to 10, then start over.

- Internally say "in" on inhalation and "out" on exhalation.

- Internally say an encouraging word or verse. One of my favorites is the first line of the poem "Desiderata" by Max Ehrmann: On inhale I silently say, "Go placidly" and on exhale, "amid the noise and haste."[1]

*Positive Imagery.* If you've already created a positive imagery practice for yourself (see Chapter 5), sitting in the chemo chair is the perfect time to do it. The more often you tap into your personal imagery, the better. With repetition, it becomes easier and easier to access these positive feelings and to steep the brain in them.

Close your eyes. Relax your facial muscles, shoulders, arms, hands, and so on down the body.

Bring your healing images to mind. Keep focusing on them, including as many senses in the visualization as you can: sights, sounds, smells, tastes, tactile sensations.

*Take Your Memory Out for a Jog.* Some people love trivia. If that's you, it can help to focus on things in your memory bank to keep yourself occupied. Choose topics that you are interested in, so it doesn't feel like a chore! Here are some suggestions:

- Run through the states in your mind. See if you can name them alphabetically. Then try the capitals!

- Recall as many of your teachers' names as possible. See if you can get them in chronological order.

- Name as many US presidents as you can. Extra points for getting them in order!

- Name the elements in the periodic table.

- Name as many Broadway shows as you can.

- Recall as many country song titles as you can.

## HOW OTHERS CAN HELP

Certainly, you can enlist whoever accompanies you to chemo to help you pass the time in a way that makes you feel most comfortable. It could be just sitting with you quietly as you listen to music, or engaging in any sort of game or activity that can be done easily as you receive your chemo dose. And of course, you need someone there who can provide whatever snack you may crave at any moment!

# CHAPTER 7

# HELLO NAUSEA, HOW ARE YOU TODAY?

On the first day or two after each round of chemo I felt okay. Tired and foggy, but upright. The steroids I was prescribed right before and after treatment were pretty powerful at keeping the nausea at bay. But the third day was a different story. I called days three through ten "sofa days."

I would wake up to the ever-present aroma of Andy's coffee (which, thankfully, didn't add to my nausea). In a semi-upright position, I brushed my teeth, put on clothes that were one step up from pajamas, and shuffled downstairs to the sofa. All of that took incredible determination and a surprising amount of time. In my mind's eye, I would see the blue sofa in the family room: my goal, my reward at the end of enormous effort!

Soon, Andy came down from his makeshift office in my son's old bedroom and poked his head into the family room.

"Good morning, honey!" Andy has one volume level: enthusiastic. "Can I get you toast and tea on this wonderful morning?"

I nodded with my eyes closed.

I was so wiped out I couldn't even specify that I liked the toast almost, but not quite, burnt, and wanted the merest hint of milk in my tea. Chemo had stripped me of my capacity to care, even to gather any semblance of thought about caring. All day long I accepted sustenance in whatever form Andy presented it. Too much chicken noodle soup in the bowl so it sloshed over the rim. Too many saltines next to the soup (*I'll never eat all of those. And just thinking of saltines makes me more nauseous.*). I heard him banging around in the kitchen, feeding the cats, washing dishes, *doing things his way*. From my spot on the sofa, I couldn't say a word. I was cured, if temporarily, of my "particular-ness," as Andy put it.

It took two rounds of chemo, which equaled four weeks, to figure out that the thing which helped quell the nausea most was not any of the three medications that my oncologist had prescribed. It was CBD oil, which my friend, Leslie, had given me. But in those four weeks—I think of them as "B-CBD" (before

CBD)—my old friend Nausea and I got reacquainted. We'd spent many months together when I was pregnant with each of my kids, over twenty years before. With my first pregnancy I spent five months bemoaning, *When will this nausea end?* With my second, I took a bright-side view: *Each day is one day closer to when this nausea will end.* I can honestly say that the severity of morning sickness was just as bad as chemo nausea. The difference, I suppose, was in the story attached. My morning sickness ended each time with a beautiful baby. Chemo sickness ends with … who knows? In the grip of that particular nausea, it was hard work to continually remind myself *this, too, shall pass.* Ten days after the first chemo treatment, I wrote in my journal:

> *I don't want to be attached to symptoms like nausea or headache, or to obsess over them. I need forbearance to keep from falling into the trap of equating these symptoms with who I am.*

My old friend Nausea had an insidious nature. It nagged relentlessly. It goaded me into trying to stop it or escape from it. And when I was in its grip, I wasn't at the top of my game. But somehow, from my fetal position on the family room sofa, I knew I didn't want to get sucked into the broken record of *when will I feel better?* I wanted to stay the course I had set before starting chemo, remaining positive, and keeping what was going on in my mind productive and nourishing.

I couldn't stop the nausea completely, but I could learn to live with it. I tried to follow the suggestion of Thict Nhat Hanh, the great Vietnamese Buddhist monk, who wrote that in order to rise out of sadness or adversity, we can make friends with the situation.[1] Greet it each day: *Hello, Nausea. How are you today?* In this way, we can see ourselves in relationship to the condition, and maybe recognize any tendency to attach our very existence to it. Only once we see that relationship can we also see that, in fact, who we are is separate from any symptom or condition.

> ## "At any moment, you have a choice that either leads you closer to your spirit or further away from it."
> ### THICH NHAT HANH

In the B-CBD days, I tried each medication my doctor had prescribed, although none made a dent in the sick feeling that ran from my brain to my gut and back again. To distract myself, I watched nostalgic sitcoms like *Rhoda* and *Designing Women* to soften the edges on long days. And I came up with a few "yoga snacks" (mini yoga exercises, as opposed

delicious treats!) to help me survive the time on the couch. I often did these yoga snacks in increments of one minute. On those days, that's what I needed—to pass the time, minute-by-minute, without getting swept up in thinking that the nausea was a symbol of anything more than nausea. And when you need all the strength you can muster just to *think* about getting up and taking 15 steps to the bathroom, you're at risk of dropping into some pretty nonproductive thinking! It's easy to spiral into, *What is my life?* on days three through ten after chemo. In fact, it was hard work to stay out of the self-pity zone. I felt so fatigued and sick to my core that I really had to stay conscious of putting one foot in front of the other on the way to the bathroom and not get sidelined by fear and doubt.

I was lucky to have the gift of yoga for those moments. I remembered my own breath and tuned into it as a focal point. *I'm breathing in. I'm breathing out.* It helped me stay in the here-and-now, just as it had done when I was in the chemo chair at Sloan-Kettering. It helped me steer clear of big "what if's" and kept me anchored in the mundane truth of, *Yup. I'm walking to the bathroom now. That's what's happening.*

## HOW YOGA HELPED

Here are the yoga snacks I used on the sofa. If you're going through chemo, maybe these will help you too. You can do them throughout the day, as tolerated. Please know that there were some days when I couldn't even muster the brain power it took to think, *Hey, I should do those yoga snacks I came up with.*

You really have to be gentle with yourself if you're going through this. Whatever you can manage is good enough. On days when I just couldn't lift a finger or take a mildly deep breath, I told myself, *You'll be able to do it on another day. You have reserves that are inside you, and that strength will come back.*

### Sofa Yoga Snack 1: "Opposite Finger/Toe Stretch"

You can do this exercise in any comfortable position. If you're like me, you'll most likely be in the fetal position!

- Breathe softly. Sometimes trying to breathe deeply makes you feel more nauseous, so stay at a level that comforts you.

- As you breathe in, slowly stretch the fingers of your right hand and the toes of your left foot. It's okay if they barely move. As you breathe out, relax them.

- Repeat this with the left fingers and right toes.

- Then inhale and stretch all 10 fingers and toes. On exhale relax them.

- That's one set. You can do it just one time or a couple times, whatever you can manage. I also enjoyed gently rocking my body back and forth as I did this.

### Sofa Yoga Snack 2: "Left Inhale/Right Exhale"

This breath technique calms and sedates the autonomic nervous system, which gets ramped up when we feel nauseous. You can do it in any position; you'll just need to be able to bring one hand to your nostrils for alternate blocking as you breathe (see also Chapter 2). *Breathe smoothly and calmly throughout.*

- Use the right thumb and ring finger to partially block both nostrils just below the bridge of the nose.

- Now fully block the right nostril with the thumb and inhale through the partially-blocked left.

- Then fully block the left nostril with the ring finger and exhale through the partially-blocked right.

- Keep repeating the same pattern, **inhale left, exhale right.** *(Note: Going in the other direction, inhaling right, exhaling left, is quite stimulating for the nervous system, and it is not recommended unless instructed by a skilled teacher for a specific purpose.)*

- Try to do it for 2–5 minutes. If that's too long, just do as many rounds as you can.

### Sofa Yoga Snack 3: "Open Belly"

A natural inclination during nausea is to curl up. It's a protective position prompted by the fight-flight-freeze response. But over many days of the fetal position, my belly began to feel tense. So occasionally I tried to straighten myself out to relieve the tension.

- Lying on your side against the back of the sofa, experiment with straightening your spine and taking your knees a bit further away from the belly so there is a little more "open space" in the torso.

- If the belly still feels sensitive, try taking very gentle breaths at the chest rather than trying to expand the belly on inhalation (opposite of a "belly breath"). This seems counterintuitive, because consciously expanding the belly on inhalation is associated with calming the nervous system. All I can tell you is that on those sofa days, I just couldn't take belly breaths. See what works for you. More than any other time during treatment, I considered chemo to be a time for "whatever works."

- Stay for as long as it remains comfortable. Inevitably my body wanted to return to the fetal position. But I usually felt better after opening up some space in this way.

## HOW OTHERS CAN HELP

This is definitely an opportunity for a loved one or friend to help you, *if* you so choose. For me, I like to be left alone in the inner doom of my nausea. But you may appreciate having someone lead you through the exercises above. It may help distract you in a good way. The deciding factor for me was, *How much energy do I have to expend on engaging with another person right now?* You don't want to feel any sort of need to put on a good show for anyone. Ask someone to help who can be calm and balanced while you're feeling, and perhaps looking, your crappiest.

# CHAPTER 8

# EXERCISING MY RIGHTS

On the day I started chemo, my oncologist mentioned I might be eligible for a clinical trial at Sloan-Kettering. The trial was studying how exercise during chemotherapy affects outcomes in breast cancer patients. They delivered a smart treadmill to your home, and an exercise physiologist monitored your exercise virtually. I was trying to picture myself crawling on hands and knees on a treadmill, which was about all I expected I could manage while on chemo. But my personal researcher, otherwise known as Andy, had read numerous articles saying exercise was essential for recovering from cancer.[1] So, I decided to look into joining the study.[2] Maybe I would beat the expected nausea after all.

I started to get excited about taking part in research that could help other people. Plus, I'd have a clinical team supervising my exercise. There seemed to be no downside. Two weeks later when Andy and I drove ninety minutes from suburban New Jersey to Memorial Sloan-Kettering in Manhattan for my screening appointment, I discovered the downside.

First of all, I had already started chemo. Most people are screened before they start, and for good

reason. I had to fast for eight hours before arriving—no food or drink other than water. If you've ever been on chemo, you know the misery of feeling nauseous but still wanting, no, *needing*, to eat. My appointment was at 11:30 A.M., which meant the last time I could eat something was 3:30 A.M. Which I did! My understanding was that I could eat a snack after having my blood drawn when I arrived. All I could think about during the car ride was the peanut butter sandwich and sports drink packed in my tote bag. I just had to make it there and then I could have that snack.

After having my blood drawn, I asked the technician, "Can I eat my snack now?"

She said, "No, I don't think you can eat anything yet."

I didn't like her after that.

I was introduced to two oncology exercise physiologists, Dave and Kelly, who were conducting the intake. They were young and gracious. I thought about all the women with breast cancer they'd probably met over the several years of this study, all the stories they may have heard. I admired their commitment to this kind of work at such a young age. Dave reminded me of my son, who was just 25. Kelly was maybe 30.

"Nice to meet you," I said. "Can I eat my snack now?"

They apologized and said I couldn't eat until a number of tests were complete, which could take up to two hours. *Two hours?* I nearly cried right there. Part of me knew it was crazy to keep going with this. My body needed nourishment, *now.* But since I'd come this far, I might as well keep trying. They led me into a small, windowless room with an exam table, a treadmill, and other pieces of equipment.

After ninety minutes of paperwork and tests to collect cardiovascular data, I was finally, thankfully, blessedly, allowed to eat something. Dave and Kelly left me alone in the exam room for a few minutes while I ate my sandwich and gulped my electrolyte drink. They had even given me a granola bar when I checked in, bless their hearts, which I devoured.

As I sat on the edge of the exam table, wearing a paper cape which provided zero warmth against the air conditioning, I felt suddenly overwhelmed. My mind started racing. *How did I get here? No, really. How am I here, in this place, in this condition?* It felt like whiplash, then tumbling. This was October 2019. Three

months earlier I had been relaxing at the beach with my daughter Emma. In August, my routine mammogram led to a follow-up biopsy. Then more appointments, decision-making, surgery, recovery, the first round of chemo, the sofa … and now, here.

My hands were shaking from low blood sugar. As I went to throw away the granola bar wrapper, I caught sight of myself in a mirror, which I realized was thoughtfully hung there for patients. My newly-shaved head was covered in a Life is Good hat. And not in a cute kind of way. The thing is, when you lose your hair, hats are too big, so the proportions are off and you look a little odd. My skin was thin and pallid. I looked like my mom when she was sick with brain cancer. That realization brought up old thoughts, which quickly turned to tightness in my belly. I remembered the day I realized my mom was actually going to die, and how my head swam and my stomach dropped. For months after she passed away, I would remind myself that just because she'd died at 58 didn't mean I would, too. Yet, here I was, now nearly 58 myself and dealing with the thing my mom had feared most—cancer. Years of being told I looked just like my mom and sounded like her and acted like her. That all came up.

## I started doing a yoga breathing exercise to quell the anxiety: three short "sips" of breath in, then a long slow breath out through pursed lips.

The tightness in my belly began to rise to my chest and throat. I recognized what was happening. This was anxiety, skirting around my brain. I didn't want to spiral downward, at least not here, in this cold

little room. I started doing a yoga breathing exercise to quell the anxiety: three short "sips" of breath in, then a long slow breath out through pursed lips. After about ten breaths I started to feel better. I talked to myself: *I am not Mom. I'm not reliving her exact experience. This moment is not everything all at once. It's just now. If Mom were here she'd tell me that I'm strong and I can get through this.* Gradually the tightness in the chest and belly eased up. My breath slowed down and I felt calmer and a little steadier.

I wish I'd known about how yoga can help with physiological and emotional issues when my mom was going through cancer. That was before I studied yoga therapy, and at the time I still thought of yoga as just "postures." I can imagine my mom trying out the same kinds of body and breath exercises and meditation that were helping me now. But she had her own version of that support system. She was connected to her spirituality in a quiet way, and I know she spent time thinking about the big picture. My mom read a lot, topics ranging from psychology to theology to physics. She gave me a book about mindfulness and another about meditation and said she thought I might like them. So she was looking into systems beyond the Western model. After her first bout of cancer, during a four-year remission, she wrote an essay for a small newsletter, *Religion in American Life*, published in Princeton, New Jersey, where she and my step-dad lived. Her essay, "Prayer, Medical Science, and Cancer,"[3] was about the relationship between healing and faith. She wrote about the first moment she'd learned she had a brain tumor:

*I felt claustrophobic and sick at my stomach. Something had to give. Maybe I would explode, or perhaps this was happening to someone in another life. Indeed, I was experiencing the most defining of human experiences: the certainty of my own mortality.*

I can't say that I ever felt the same punch-to-the-gut moment that my mom describes here at any point throughout my cancer experience. But I didn't have to deal with the kind of diagnosis she did. She was hearing *Astrocytoma Grade IV.* I was hearing *breast cancer,* which, by statistics, has a much higher survival rate. Still, in the overly air-conditioned exercise screening room at Sloan-Kettering, I got a tiny glimpse of that "most defining of human experiences" she described.

In her essay, my mom went on to talk about the rising evidence that *"religious beliefs, faith, and prayer are major factors in healing."* She cited researchers who posited, by way of quantum physics, that everything in the universe is interconnected, and others who studied the health effects of Transcendental Meditation. One of those researchers, Herbert Benson, wrote about the plausibility of a *"link between objective science and the power of belief."*[4] Certainly, my mom's experience up to that point was bearing out the notion. She wrote,

*I have a deep sense that the tone was set for healing through my prayers, and through the concerns and prayers of others on my behalf. But I am also enough of a student of science to know that the treatment was a crucial part of the process. I like to think that the "miracle" was in finding the right doctor and the right treatment for me. Most often, at least in my experience, prayer works like that.*

At the time my mom wrote this, she was cancer-free, after a first round of surgery and radiation. So, she is certainly talking about "healing" in the obvious sense of the word. But I believe as her experience marched toward what she suspected would be the inevitable return of the cancer, she found healing in another sense. Healing the trauma of that moment of mortal knowing. Healing that wound so it wouldn't get in the way of her fuller inner journey.

My mom's words foreshadowed my own thoughts. I knew I wasn't going to get better without heavy drugs. But just as importantly, I knew that the continuous flow of love coming to me from so many people was just as powerful in a different way. That was the thing I held inside me and carried around with me. Every day I went to my yoga altar and soaked up those healing vibrations, steeping myself in the mystery of the energy being directed at me. After all, what are thoughts? What are prayers? What is love? Outside of a dictionary definition or a scientific explanation, I'd say they are energy. Through that practice I came to understand what persistent faith was all about. It's an *act*, not a notion. You have to keep at it, consciously. Keep your thoughts, your energy, pointed in a positive direction. In my mom's words, you have to "set the tone for healing."

By the time Dave and Kelly came back to start the next phase of the screening process—the treadmill test—I was ready to keep going. It's amazing how we can rise to an occasion, even when it probably makes no sense.

Dave attached EKG cables to a number of electrodes on my torso. Next, he strapped a large breathing device around my head. I had to get my lips entirely around the huge mouthpiece. Then, he put a large clip on my nose, which forced me to breathe though my mouth. He warned me that drool would run down my chin but not to worry about it. *Sure, let's add some uncontrolled drooling to this day. Why not?* The plan was they would slowly increase the speed and incline of the treadmill until I gave the thumbs-down sign,

which meant *Stop!—I can't go on*. Given the fact that I needed to concentrate really hard on staying relaxed since my nose was clipped shut, I expected to give the thumbs-down pretty early in the game.

"Ready to go, Julie? You're doing great so far!"

*Honestly? We haven't even started yet, but okay, thanks.* I gave the thumbs up.

The treadmill started slowly. As I walked and drooled, Kelly asked me questions about the intensity of the workout, to which I nodded or shook my head. After ten minutes and only a couple increases in speed and incline, she suddenly stopped the treadmill.

"We're seeing something we don't like, so we'll just stop for now and have it checked out."

I checked my reaction. *Okay, let's not panic, let's just find out what this is.* I could feel myself working to stay in the wait-and-see mindset, mentally nudging aside any what-if thoughts that bubbled up. And thank goodness Dave took the headgear off so I could actually breathe. I noticed myself smiling at the two of them and realized I was doing what a natural-born people pleaser does. *It's okay, you two kids. It's gonna be fine. You're doing great.*

What happened next was an example of why I was so glad I'd gone to a fully-integrated cancer center like Sloan Kettering for my treatment. Kelly picked up the phone and punched in an extension. Within one minute she was talking to a cardiologist who was looking at my EKG from the treadmill test.

She hung up and said, "It's a benign reaction. We can keep going."

She gave a more scientific summary to Dave, which I understood somewhat—I'd been part of a cardiac rehabilitation team at one point, providing stress management through yoga to cardiac patients. In my case, the EKG was showing a slight arhythmic-beat pattern, which is not unusual. But they had to be sure.

We repeated the process and got to about 15 minutes of exercise, which was no picnic. I didn't feel I'd recovered my glucose levels after my snack, so I was pushing the limit of my stamina. All along, I soothed myself with the knowledge that I could give the thumbs-down whenever I wanted. These people were not the boss of me! Once this intake nonsense was over and I was in the study, I would just start out my personal exercise program at the lowest level. I'd do ten minutes at a snail's pace on their state-of-the-art treadmill in my living room. That was fine with me. I didn't have anything to prove.

Suddenly Kelly and Dave exchanged looks. "We're going to stop you again, Julie. You're doing great, but we just want to make sure everything is still safe."

I was happy to oblige by stopping the treadmill and taking off the drool mask. Once again, I worked at remaining reaction-free, and realized I was channeling my paternal grandmother, Nana Mest, as I'd done a few other times lately. Just smiling and waiting.

The answer from the cardiologist came back the same: Okay to continue exercising.

*That's what they think.*

Apparently, my inner power had come to life. It was two o'clock in the afternoon. I'd been at this appointment for three hours. Even after my snack, I was still undernourished, and more importantly, had a low white cell blood count from the first chemo treatment 12 days prior. When Dave said they hadn't captured enough data to enter me into the study, and I still needed to get to maximum cardiac output on the treadmill, I said, "Nope."

They said I could come back and try the next

morning. I wouldn't need to fast again. That would be the last chance to get into the study. I thought about it. Driving into the city again, dealing with the crowds while trying to avoid germs to protect my depleted immune system, all so I could pant and drool and push myself to physical failure on a treadmill.

My body was telling me in no uncertain terms, "No." My inner voice agreed. I had a few moments of regret before letting go of the idea of being part of the clinical study. Then I turned my attention to what really mattered: *lunch.*

As Andy and I drove home, and I was finally feeling human again after a real meal at a bistro across from the hospital, we talked about the takeaway from the day. I would try to exercise as much as I could manage. At my next chemotherapy appointment, I told Dr. A. about the experience. She said, "Of course you couldn't do that test. You had a low white cell count. They should have realized that." Her corroboration made me feel better, although honestly, by that point I knew that much of what would spur my inner healing would come from my own decisions, my own choices, based on what I alone knew. Plus, she had been the one who had suggested the trial, after I'd already started chemo! *Okay, no one's perfect.*

The next week, Andy set up a stationary bike in the family room, right next to the blue sofa. The first few days after chemo treatments were always too rough to do any exercise, but by day six or so I would will myself off the sofa and onto the bike. I'd pedal for 15 minutes (remarkably slowly!), leaning over the handle bars, nauseous, watching my sitcoms. Having the bike right there made it easy to do some sort of exercise at a moment's notice.

Andy and I went for walks, short ones at first,

bundled up against winter days. One time, we went to a stone-paved labyrinth at a convent not far from my house. I had first encountered a labyrinth at another convent, the one in California where I'd found my candle holder inscribed with St. Julian's quotation: *All shall be well, and all shall be well, and all manner of thing shall be well.* There was a sign at the entrance to that labyrinth which explained how to walk through it. The idea is you start at the beginning with whatever you are carrying—a burden, a worry, a question. You walk slowly, following the winding path of paved stones to the center. There you "put down" whatever you carried in. Some people place small stones or flowers or other trinkets there as symbols of their burden. Then, you continue following the stones as they wind back and forth, eventually leading you out again, maybe a bit lighter in heart and mind.

The first time we went to walk the labyrinth near my home in New Jersey, it was covered in leaves, making it impossible to see the path. The next time, Andy pulled a broom out of the trunk and went in front of me, sweeping away the leaves so I could follow the design to the center and back out again. (The happy problem-solver at it again!) It was a simple exercise, took about twenty minutes. But it was an accomplishment.

There was usually at least one day between chemo treatments when I could attempt a longer walk. On those days we went to a nearby national historical park, Jockey Hollow, with a two-mile paved road that included several hills. I loved being out in nature, in the fresh air, among the tall trees. The first time we did that walk I wasn't sure I would make it! We slowed down to a laughable pace on the hills, even stopping so I could catch my breath. I couldn't really hold a conversation, because all of my physical and mental effort was channeled into putting one foot in front of the other. I can't say how important it was to have had Andy there, just walking along, chatting away. He knew it was hard, but he was always monitoring how I was doing. I knew he'd carry me back to the car if necessary, which gave me the confidence to keep going.

By the time I finished chemo months later, we probably walked that road and those hills ten times. It remained hard all the way through. I got used to the sensation of shortness of breath, and, in the process, gained invaluable respect for my cardiovascular system. Never again would I take my physical condition for granted. Ultimately, whether I was part of a clinical trial or not, I know that keeping active, at any pace, contributed to my recovery.

## HOW YOGA HELPED

Figuring out the right exercise for me during cancer treatment involved some ups and downs, physically and emotionally. I reached into my yoga toolkit for the exercises below to help manage the physical and emotional symptoms at different points along the way.

# RELAX WITH YOUR BREATH (SEE ALSO CHAPTERS 2 AND 9)

1. Begin by lying on your stomach on the floor, if possible. Fold the arms, resting your head on your forearms. Position the arms so the base of your ribcage touches the floor, but the upper chest is away from the floor. If it is not possible to lie on your stomach, lie on your back instead.

2. On inhale, feel your abdomen expand and press against the floor as your back gently rises.

3. On exhale, feel the abdomen relax as the back gently falls.

4. Keep your attention softly focused on the sensations of each breath. Let the body relax completely.

5. Stay for 5–10 minutes. Then slowly sit up. Notice the ease of your breathing and your state of mind.

6. If you are not in a place where you can lie down, you can do this exercise sitting up. Place your hands on your belly to feel the expansion and relaxation of the abdomen as you breathe.

## "SIPPING BREATH" TO CALM ANXIETY (SEE ALSO CHAPTER 13)

This exercise works by starting out "where you are" when you are anxious, which is often with short, shallow inhalations. The "sipping" technique allows you to take what is comfortable at that moment—just a short little inhalation. But taking three sips gets more air into your lungs than one short, shallow breath. At the same time, the pursed-lip technique lengthens the exhalation, signaling the brain to switch from flight-flight-freeze mode to rest-digest-relax mode. Eventually, your body is ready to stretch the inhalation, so you can decrease to two sips. And finally, as flight-fight-freeze subsides, you are ready for one smooth inhalation and exhalation.

Use this breath exercise when you start to feel anxious. For me, the first sign of anxiety is tightness in my belly. There are many other signs, like shallow or "choppy" breathing, elevated pulse, digestive upset, clenched jaw, buzzing in the ears, racing thoughts, just to mention a few.

*Although it is unlikely, if at any time while you are doing this technique you feel more anxious, light-headed, or dizzy, stop and breathe in any way that comes naturally.* You know your own body best, so follow your instincts.

### Instructions

1. **Inhale in 3 little "sips,"** followed by a long exhalation through pursed lips, as if you're playing the flute. Let the sips be slow and smooth, rather than quick and sharp. Notice your belly draws inward when you exhale. Then, on the next set of inhale sips, let your belly expand out again.

2. **Continue for about 5 rounds.** Then pause and take a few "natural" breaths, with no specific technique. I find it best to take breaks after a few rounds; otherwise, I feel a little lightheaded.

3. Then, **take 2 sips** to inhale and exhale through pursed lips.

4. **Continue for about 5 rounds.** Then pause and take a few "natural" breaths, with no specific technique.

5. If you are feeling calmer, shift to **1 smooth inhalation.** Exhale slowly and smoothly, **this time through the nose** instead of through pursed lips.

6. After 5 rounds, notice how you feel: your body, your breath, your mind. If you still feel anxious, you can repeat the process.

### Working with Shortness of Breath (SOB)

This was one of the most prevalent symptoms I experienced while on chemo (along with my companion, Nausea). Suddenly, all kinds of things were hard to do. It took me a little time to figure out how to deal with shortness of breath, but here's what I ended up with:

*Overall, I slowed down everything, including:*

- transitions from lying to sitting, sitting to standing, standing to walking

- going up stairs

- movements when doing a task, like laundry, emptying the dishwasher, even dressing or undressing.

*I made these adjustments to my yoga practice:*

- Remained down on the floor for the entire practice.

- "Deconstructed" the postures until I was working in micro-movements. For example, instead of lifting my chest and head off the floor in a "cobra" position, I just elongated my spine and expanded my chest ever so slightly.

- Used fewer repetitions of each posture.

- Eliminated any postures that felt too taxing that day.

- Decreased the length of breath in and out.

- Whispered the chant instead of chanting out loud.

- Took a break for several moments between postures.

- I pedaled on my stationary bike like a sloth in slow motion. But the mental boost I got from doing a little exercise was vital!

- On walks, especially where there was a hill, I slowed down to a snail's pace. I have to thank Andy for this piece of common-sense advice. He'd enlightened me on this topic when we first met and were on my first "real" hike up a bonafide mountain. He also suggested not talking, a real challenge for me! But conserving all of my cardiovascular output for nothing more than putting one foot slowly in front of the other really worked. I could make it up hills, still feeling the exertion but not becoming overwhelmed.

- Most importantly, I kept telling myself, *This SOB is temporary. Even though I hate it, it's a reminder to take good care of myself.*

## HOW OTHERS CAN HELP

Friends love to help, so ask them to do whatever exercise you feel up for. They could pick you up and take you to a nice spot for a walk. Be sure to explain how you're doing that day. For instance, when my friends would go for walks with me, I had to explain about the shortness of breath so they wouldn't get worried about how slowly I was moving!

# CHAPTER 9

# HAIR TODAY, GONE TODAY

One week after my first chemo treatment, I spent three days in the hospital, the result of picking up a virus and spiking a fever. When you're on chemo, your white blood cell count is drastically low, so if you get a fever that exceeds about 101° it's imperative to find out if the fever is due to an infection. A viral infection is not so bad because it will generally run its course. But a bacterial infection can enter the bloodstream, and that's very bad.

It took three days waiting for blood test cultures to determine that my infection was viral, which was good news. On one of those days, I was finally allowed some time off the precautionary antibiotic IV long enough to take a shower. It took a minute for me to realize that thick clumps of hair were coming off in my hands as I lathered my head with shampoo. I'd certainly read about when and how hair loss happens on chemo, so I wasn't surprised. Actually, I was relieved. Finally, this iconic passage that I knew was coming had arrived. Now I could deal with it.

For the next few days, I walked around like Charlie Brown's Christmas tree, dropping needles everywhere. At one point I was brushing my hair after a shower, and with each pass more and more hair came out. Soon I had a pile of hair on the bathroom counter that I swear was equal to the amount that was still on my head! I called Andy in to take a look and we both cracked up. It was one of those absurd moments that for us was much better to laugh at than to cry about.

"Let's do it," I said.

I spread a large towel on the bathroom floor and set a kitchen stool on top. Andy got out the electric razor he uses to shave his head daily. Within five minutes, I was hair-free. Or at least close. I ran my hand over my head. "Stubby" might have been a good nickname! It looked and felt weird to be bald, but this meant I was moving forward. I swept up the hair and threw it away, with the exception of a small clump, which I put into a plastic bag. I'd read that if you wanted to buy a wig, it was best to send a tuft of your real hair to match the color (not that my hair was my "real" color—it hadn't been real for many years!). I didn't expect to wear a wig and never ended up ordering one, but I saved the hair, just in case.

A few weeks earlier, I'd begun to prepare for my baldness like any self-respecting consumer: by purchasing lots of hats. I had Newsie caps, baseball caps, beanies, even a woolen Nordic princess hat complete with knitted Viking helmet horns and ponytails! That one actually looked pretty good, and I figured out why—even though the ponytails were made out of yarn, they still gave the impression of having hair.

THE VIKING PRINCESS ACTUALLY LOOKED PRETTY GOOD!

Several of the other hats were also designed to give the illusion that you had hair. They did this mostly be being a bit fuller at the back or on top. On me all this did was make it look like the hats were too big at the back or on top!

Other camouflaging tricks I had read about were covering the head with a scarf or pulling your hat all the way down over the base of the skull. When the base of the skull shows below a hat, it looks different than on someone who might just have a super-short haircut but still has hair on the nape of the neck.

I even tried the combination scarf-under-baseball cap. It was a bit like Soccer Mom Meets Rhoda Morgenstern. Not a winner.

SCARF UNDER BASEBALL CAP: FAIL.

I decided to try ordering a kid-sized hat, since one problem I had was that adult hats were just too big. The result: I looked like an adult wearing a kid-sized hat.

Eventually, I settled on a winter hat that I'd had for a few years. It was a bit big on my bald head, so I added a jersey-knit hat liner (check out Headcoverings.com), which provided just enough extra width to keep the hat from dropping down over my eyes. I ended up wearing that hat almost every day for seven months. It was just the right size and shape for my head, and just the right "day look" for me.

Then there were my nightcaps. Suddenly, I could

**SOMEWHERE A TODDLER IS MISSING HER HAT!**

**THE GOLDILOCKS PERFORMER**

relate to "Mama in her kerchief and I in my cap" from Clement C. Moore's poem, "The Night Before Christmas." When you're bald, a hat keeps you warm at night! But it took a little trial and error to find one that wasn't *too* warm. One of my staples was a blue terrycloth turban-style number. That one fell into the category of *"I've become my mom."* Not only was it the kind of thing my mother wore when she was going through cancer, but I could picture us laughing together at how unflattering it was (you'll notice there's no photo evidence of that one!), and how little we cared. The blue turban was a Goldilocks performer, neither too hot nor too cold for sleeping.

But my favorite nighttime caps were hand-knit in soft velour yarn by my very dear friend, Sue. She belonged to a group that knitted and donated caps to chemo patients. She sent me at least six caps in different colors, using a child-sized knitting loom so they fit perfectly. These were my cozy, after-dinner, TV-watching, pajama-time hats, all the more comforting because they came from Sue. I will always be thankful for the love she knitted into them.

Losing the hair on my head was one part of the experience. Then there were the eyebrows and eyelashes. You don't realize how much these features create the look of what we think of as a "normal" face until you don't have them. The drug I took for the last two months of chemo, Taxol, slowly wiped out all body hair. This is great for legs and armpits. But as the weeks went on, my head and face became smooth and shiny, almost featureless.

The issue of appearance was something of a seesaw for me. I knew the way I looked was a result of the medicine, and I didn't want to get caught up in bemoaning my appearance. I understood then and now that my appearance is not who I truly am. This truth is at the heart of what I know from yoga. The body is a temporary home for an abiding spirit.

When I practice yoga, I can glimpse that spirit, some-times fleetingly, sometimes for longer. I don't say that lightly—it's a *felt* sense, a connection to an ineffable life force, that often arises after taking time to center my attention and quiet my mind. Of course, glimps-ing, even on a semi-routine basis, is a long way off from living full time as a self-realized being who is unattached to her external form.

So, for the work-in-progress yogi that is me, look-ing in the mirror and seeing a wan complexion with no hair, eyebrows, or eyelashes was a bit of a bummer at times. Some days it was hard to maintain the posi-tive mindset I knew was crucial to healing. Also, there was a part of me that wanted the people around me—my kids, my sister, my friends, Andy—not to have to see me looking quite so bad. I think this reaction can be common among women in particular: *Let me worry about this so you don't have to.* I know full well that was my own projection; none of them needed me to protect them.

In the midst of these conflicting thoughts and feel-ings about appearance, I found that wearing a little make-up every day made me feel better. I've always loved wearing make-up, so why stop now? It helped me keep a "one-day-closer-to-renewed-health" atti-tude. My morning make-up routine was pretty com-ical, looking back on it. I continued to brush the lightest coat of mascara on my thinning eyelashes, until they were literally all gone. My eyebrows slowly shrunk, and each morning I counted the few remain-ing stragglers. Emma bought me an eyebrow pencil, which I used to "feather" in the illusion of fuller brows. Wearing glasses was an advantage because they par-tially obscured my brows anyway, and offered a visual outline above my eyes. One day, I realized the nine remaining eyebrow hairs (yes, I could count them indi-vidually by the light of my 10x-magnification mirror!) were barely hanging on, and when I touched them—poof—they were gone.

What I was doing each morning when I looked in the mirror was an emotional balancing act. On the one hand, a little obsession. When I think of how many days in a row I counted the individual eyelashes! And for what? Nothing was going to change! On the other hand, a little cheerleading. *Come on hair, I know you can do it. You were made to grow, and you'll grow again!* And when I balanced in the middle, I knew all of that had nothing to do with *me.* I knew in my heart the most important part of me never changes.

And yet.

When the day rolled around that I discovered one little hair on the side of my head that was a scintilla of a centimeter longer than the rest of the stubs, I admit it, I was *psyched!* Then, I saw an army of eyebrow roots gathering just beneath the surface of the skin. And three rows of tiny black dots emerging along the eyelids. Watching my eyelashes and eyebrows regrow turned out to be a pretty cool experience. Soon, they couldn't be stopped. Eyelashes appeared in the corners of my eyes where I didn't realize eyelashes would fit. My eyebrows kept growing, sprouting satellite hairs all the way around the eye socket! A soft downy cov-ering of hair appeared on my cheeks. Yikes, now I was getting what I'd asked for!

Luckily, things settled down after a few weeks, and a lot of the extra facial hair seemed to disappear. In a fun twist, a problem that I'd had for some time, long before cancer, was also resolved. No more color-ing my hair! I wanted to get out of the cycle of chas-ing after gray roots, month after month, year after year. Now Mother Nature was taking care of it for me. My new hair was salt-and-pepper and would stay that way. In yet another opportunity to see the bright side, my hair began regrowing during the COVID-19 pandemic, when the world had to stay home and hair salons were closed. Suddenly, having naturally gray hair that wouldn't need to be cut for months and months was an asset!

Those first couple months of new hair growth were great. I thought I was on my way to a fun new style I could jazz up with some funky blue or purple highlights. What I didn't count on was how the estrogen suppressant I had to take for five to ten years would affect my thick new head of hair. About a month into taking that drug, I started thinning on top. I went from obsessing over how many eyelashes I had to checking out my bald spot in the bathroom mirror. I got creative with the blow dryer, trying to camouflage the white scalp showing through. I'll be honest—it was bumming me out.

One night about a year later, Andy and I were watching *Queer Eye*. At the end of the show, they gave the woman who got a makeover a red light laser cap because she was self-conscious about her thinning hair. I sat up.

"Hey, I'm self-conscious about *my* thinning hair! What is that thing, and where can I get one?"

Andy the Researcher to the rescue. We discovered that laser caps are, indeed, an FDA-approved device shown to help regrow hair. I decided to give it a try. I will say the one I bought wasn't cheap. But, now that I didn't color my hair and only needed a cut every eight to ten weeks, the cap paid for itself quickly. The warranty on the cap required "before" photos, so I took pictures of my head the day before I started using the device. I am happy to say that within four weeks, there was less bald spot and more hair. I was gleeful! I took pictures again around eight weeks and proudly showed my friends. They couldn't believe how much it had worked. And my hair stylist was blown away (no pun intended!).

Now, friends, *please understand*: this kind of device worked for me, but I am not recommending it globally. It's a personal decision. I got lucky by spotting it on a TV show. But once I got it, I realized I could have been seeking out other solutions all along, rather than looking at my bald spot every day and wondering why it hadn't changed. I share this to encourage you to seek out solutions if you find you're not happy with something. For instance, I eventually added an over-the-counter topical hair growth solution and a daily dose of biotin (the hair, skin and nails supplement) to my routine, which also helped fill in the thin spots. There will certainly be things we can't change and have to adjust to living with. But there might be things that work. The important part is not to get attached to the outcome. The bald spot is not who I am.

Yes, even as I write that I see the problem. *Easy for you to say, Julie. You don't have a bald spot to obsess over anymore!* However, I no longer have the thick, wavy hair I used to have. And I never will. I have the kind of hair that people tend to overlook. A makeup stylist who gave me some tips before my son's wedding put it this way: "When you don't have that full head of hair, it's just your face, out there, saying, *'this is me.'*" She wasn't insulting me. She got exactly how I was feeling.

Some days, I understand what women mean when they say they feel invisible in their fifties and beyond.

It's been a journey for my hair and me. Our relationship has evolved. Some days, I really like the way it looks. Some days, I understand what women mean when they say they feel invisible in their fifties and beyond. Yoga gives me a way to frame the experience into a do-able practice, so I can keep working at it and say, "Hello, Hair. How are you today?"

## HOW YOGA HELPED

Two valuable teachings from yoga were especially helpful as I went through hair loss and regrowth:

1. **Nonattachment** (*Vairāgya* – pronounced vy RAH gya). This concept reminds us to step back and observe things dispassionately, objectively. Over time, this approach helps us to let go of the "stories" we may tell ourselves about how we look, and to remember that as much as our appearance may change, our essence never changes.

2. **Acceptance** (*Santosha*). Once we are tuned into nonattachment, a natural next step is making peace with the way things are in this moment. To accept the things that we cannot change so that we do not continue to suffer over them.

3. **Meditation.** On the following page is a meditation practice to help ride the emotions that might come with changes in appearance during cancer. It encourages cultivating an attitude of nonattachment and acceptance, and to recall that who we

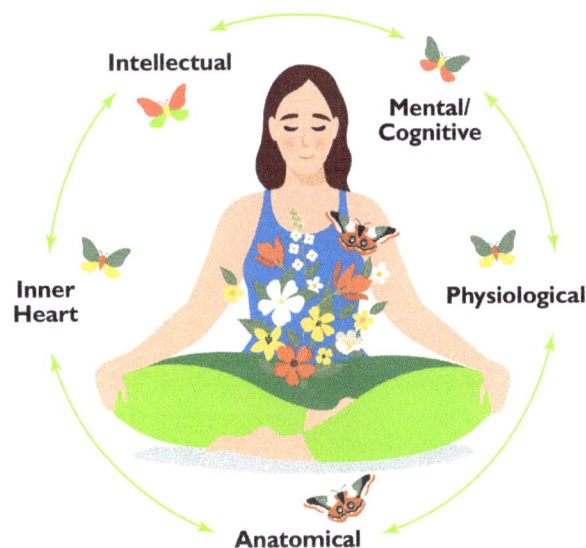

truly are never changes. You can do this meditation in a couple ways:

- Read the instructions and do each step. Don't worry about opening your eyes to look at the book—this is how I do it all the time until I learn a new practice!

- Record yourself or someone else reading the instructions, then follow along with that recording.

# MEDITATION ABOUT CHANGING APPEARANCE

### Step 1. Relax with Diaphragmatic Breathing
(see also Chapters 2, 8)

1. Begin by lying on your stomach. Fold the arms, resting your head on your forearms. Position the arms so the base of your ribcage touches the floor, but the upper chest is away from the floor. If it is not possible to lie on your stomach, lie on your back instead.

2. On inhale, feel your abdomen expand and press against the floor as your back gently rises. On exhale, feel the abdomen relax as the back falls.

3. Keep your attention softly focused on the sensations of each breath. Let the body relax completely.

4. Stay for 5 minutes, then slowly sit up; notice your breath.

### Step 2. Seated Meditation

1. Set-up

   - Sit upright on a firm cushion or straight-backed chair. Align your head over your spine.

   - Relax your facial muscles, shoulders, arms, and hands.

   - Close your eyes or lower your gaze.

2. Focus

   - Bring your attention to the tip of your nose. Feel the air flow into and out of your nostrils. Breathe slowly and smoothly.

   - Count backward from 10 to 0 on the exhales.

   - Now, bring your attention to the area of your heart. Imagine you are seated in your heart center in an "observer's chair."

3. Observe

   - Notice any emotion that arises about the effects of treatment on your appearance. Describe the feeling. Keep it simple. For instance, *I feel uncomfortable letting others see me with no hair.*

   - Watch from your "observer's chair." Let the feeling arise fully. Notice whatever accompanies it—maybe other feelings like sadness or embarrassment, or bodily sensations like shallow breathing or agitation. It may help to name each sensation as you notice it: *That's sadness.* Or, *That's shallow breathing.* These are just examples. Watch and name your own experiences. Resist going further into conversation with yourself, judging, or evaluating.

   - Continue to observe the wave of feelings and/or sensations in this way. Give it time.

   - Then, notice that in time they subside. Recognize the experience of nonattachment as you watch them go.

   - In the clear space left in the wake of the receding emotions/sensations, recognize your ability to accept the present moment. *I got through those feelings. I allowed them to come and go.*

4. Reframe Your Perspective

- Remind yourself that even though outward appearances may change, your inner essence never changes. For instance, *The love I share with others does not emanate from my hair follicles. It comes from an invisible place deep within.* Use whatever words are natural for you. Keep it simple.

- Let that truth sink in for a few moments. If it feels natural to you, offer gratitude for the ability to separate fleeting emotions from your abiding essence.

- Open your eyes and continue your day, refreshed and confident in your inner strength.

## HOW OTHERS CAN HELP

Let friends and family know your feelings about losing your hair. Enlist them to order different hats or head coverings if you don't have the energy to scour the internet or stores. Ask one of them to help you pick out a wig if you plan to wear one. Or let them know if you prefer no head covering at all. Don't feel pressured into any kind of "fix" if it's not up your alley. Keep hunting around until you find your Goldilocks solution!

## CHAPTER 10

# LET'S START A MOVEMENT

One of the side effects of chemotherapy is constipation. Some people might shy away from writing about this one, but not me. I come by it naturally. When I was a little girl, if I didn't feel well, the first thing my Nana Weinsheimer would say was, "Did your bowels move today?" It was a common topic among my mom, aunt, sister, and cousin, as well. My stepdad lovingly coined this family conversation the *Bowel Bulletin.*

I didn't realize as a kid how wise my grandmother was in this way. She was following Mother Nature's direction, which in this case was *down and out.* In *Āyurveda,* a holistic medical system which is sometimes called the "sister science" to yoga, there is a model of the human energy system which includes the downward flow of energy—it's called *apāna.* This energy governs all the things that are discharged from the physical body. You get the picture. There is even a yoga exercise named for this downward flow: *Apānāsana*— Downward Flowing Energy Pose (see photos below), where we bring the knees in and out to massage the lower belly. It's one of the most useful exercises we can do for ourselves on a daily basis.

I remember being at the doctor's office when I was young, maybe in my teens. I'm not even sure what I was there for, but it must have been related to

*APĀNĀSANA* STARTING POSITION

*APĀNĀSANA* ENDING POSITION

digestion, because the doctor suggested I pull my knees in toward my belly and then gently rock back and forth. He was giving me the same medicine that my grandmother had dispensed—follow nature's course. Bringing the knees into the belly massages the colon, and rocking side to side encourages the natural flow through the system. That's one of the few times I can ever recall a medical doctor suggesting something so natural and low-tech.

My early childhood experiences mirrored what I came to study and learn about in yoga therapy. And I was really happy to have had that training in the days right after a chemo treatment when the *Bowel Bulletin* typically read, "Closed for Business." The chemo nurses made sure I had a stool softener on hand and even suggested a laxative if necessary. "You don't want to get blocked—it's important to keep things moving so your body can shed all the drugs in your system."

After my first round of treatment, I found the stool softeners weren't enough to do the job. I hesitated taking the laxative because I felt at my limit with the drugs in my body, so I muddled through. Enough said. By the second round of chemo, I was better able to plan ahead. On the day after treatment, I was still taking strong steroids to ward off the worst nausea, which meant I would feel well enough to do some exercise. I pulled out my trusty "Practice for Constipation." I had learned this from my teacher, Gary, and went on to teach it myself to yoga therapists-in-training and several constipation sufferers. The reviews

always come back a few hours after the practice: "It worked like a charm!"

I couldn't agree more. This practice *works*. The idea is to use long, smooth exhalations in forward bending and twisting positions. The exhalations are key because when we exhale the abdomen naturally draws inward. In this practice, we consciously draw in the abdomen even further, lengthening the duration of the exhalation, and even holding the breath and belly in at some points. All of this has the effect not only of massaging the colon and encouraging the natural downward flow of energy, just like that doctor had shown me, but also turning on the "rest and digest" side of the nervous system, and turning off its opposite, "fight or flight," so you can relax about something that can both cause stress *and* be made worse by stress.

I did some version of this practice the day after each chemo treatment. To be sure, I had to slow it down, add in resting breaths, skip some of the more vigorous postures, and generally calibrate it to my current condition, but the strategy still delivered. I needed less stool softener and never took a laxative. The nurses who made the posttreatment follow-up calls were always happy to hear how smoothly things were going for me. Constipation is a big problem for some people, and I really feel for them. I was lucky to know about this practice, the effect of which is felt at the anatomical, physiological, and mental/emotional levels. That's the holistic promise of yoga, down to the most basic human function.

## HOW YOGA HELPED

You'll find a sample **practice for constipation** in Chapter 22. This practice usually works for most people within 24 hours, and when I say it works, I mean it! Go gently, *especially if you are on chemotherapy.* It's very important to rest for several minutes at the end of the practice. The body needs time to assimilate its effects, and our elimination system operates best when we are in a relaxed state.

Intellectual

Mental/Cognitive

Inner Heart

Physiological

Anatomical

## HOW OTHERS CAN HELP

Let your oncology doctor or nurses know as soon as you realize you're feeling constipated, especially if you've been taking the medication they've prescribed for constipation and it's still not working. Exercise and plenty of water are very important, but sometimes we need a multi-pronged approach!

# CHAPTER 11

# WHAT GOES UP

About two weeks after the surgery to remove the lump in my breast and three lymph nodes from my underarm, I woke up and noticed something. Up to that point, I'd maintained a mostly positive mindset, with a few moments of mild panic that were quelled by deep breathing and returning to the practicality of the present moment. This typically involved doing the tasks that moved the ball down the field, like collecting medical records, going to appointments, getting through the surgery itself and managing my post-surgery care. But on this particular morning, in the very moment of waking, just before consciously shifting my mind into "positive" gear, there was a space, an opening, where I recognized, *Yup, this is depression.*

I'd felt this sensation several years earlier when I was getting divorced, so I recognized it. The first definition of depression in the dictionary relates to mental health. But honestly, the feeling I had was more akin to other uses of the word: "a sunken place or part;" "a pressing down."[1] Something felt tamped down in me, low. I would come to have this feeling on a few specific days throughout my treatment. A couple times the sadness would come out during a meditation and

tears would stream down my face, releasing a host of other emotions that had gotten jumbled together, like fear, anxiety, loss, nostalgia, pathos, gratitude, love.

Before this time, my primary experience with depression was through my mom. She had suffered with what was probably clinical depression (the more serious, persistent form of the condition) for most of her life, but didn't have a good diagnosis or an ally in the form of a helpful therapist until she was in her late forties. That was in the 1980s when things were slowly starting to change in terms of understanding and treating depression. My mom did what many, or perhaps most, people with depression did who grew up in the mid-twentieth century—she hid it, at least from me (I believe my older sister would have a different take on that). And she probably kept a lot of the details from friends and other family members, which certainly must have made it all the harder to cope with. Even after she had found better therapy and began taking antidepressants to stabilize her mood, she still suffered, but maybe she had started to better understand the condition. I honestly don't know. I think she continued trying to protect me from a difficult situation; she didn't want me to have to know how desperate she sometimes felt.

I remember only two specific conversations with my mom about her depression. The first took place a few weeks after my first child was born. My mom had been spiraling downward for some time and eventually she decided to leave New Jersey and go to Colorado to be seen by a friend there who was a psychiatrist. Since she was pretty good at hiding the depth of her condition, and I was preoccupied with being a new parent, when she called to say she was leaving town for an undetermined amount of time, I felt both hurt (selfishly) and concerned (guiltily, after feeling selfish). What I didn't feel, I realize now, was enough alarm or the gravity of the situation. I didn't say, "Mom, what can I do for you? Tell me what's happening." I trusted her when she said she would be okay but just needed to do this. On the phone, she sounded deeply apologetic about leaving when Michael had just been born, knowing I could use some help and that she would miss precious early days with him. I assured her, despite my disappointment, that it was okay, I understood. Which I did. Our ability to juggle several emotions at once adds to their very complexity.

The other conversation I recall came several months later, when she had returned to New Jersey, but ended up checking into a hospital due to, as I learned later, suicidal thoughts. My sister and I drove to the hospital together, and took turns going in to see her while the other stayed in the car with our kids, both babies. When it was my turn to visit, I sat with my mom and could feel how much work it was for her to appear okay, normal. She apologized. Again, I reassured her. Looking back on it now, I understand her instinct to apologize. You want things to be okay for your kids.

You don't want to be a source of concern for them. Then she asked me something I know was hard for her but which she probably *had* to ask for her own peace of mind.

"Do you ever get depressed?"

I said, "I feel sad sometimes, sure."

"But is it a desperate feeling? Have you ever felt this bad, the way I do? Have you ever thought of hurting yourself?"

"No, I never have."

She was visibly relieved. It felt like I was giving her a gift.

And in the way mothers do, she gave me a gift in turn. By shining a light on the experience of depression at varying degrees, she educated me. I knew that morning a few weeks after my surgery that the depression I felt was the temporary kind, the result of some very obvious, recent events. And I also knew that I didn't want to give in to it, to let the sunken place keep pressing down on my heart and my mind. I thought of my favorite quotation from Thich Nhat Hanh, "Hello, grief, how are you today?" (the same one I'd adapted to greet my friend Nausea).[2] His point was that we need to acknowledge and accept, even embrace, whatever feelings come up. Then we can work with them.

One strategy, among others, for coping with depression that I'd learned from yoga therapy was to employ the opposite feeling, energetically: a strong, vigorous yoga practice, or any exercise, to lift up what had sunk down. On this particular morning I turned to a recording of my teacher, Gary, leading a practice that centered on the theme of light (see Resources at end of the book). Like my go-to "*Durgā* Practice," this one also combined a chant with the yoga movements and breath. The chant used in this particular practice meant "filled with light." Repeating the chant throughout the practice is intended to invoke a felt sense of lightness, as opposed to heaviness, to counter that pressing down feeling that comes with a depressed mood. The meditation at the end of the practice offered the opportunity to shift perspective, to recognize the "tone" of our mindset, why it may be that way, and then choose what we want to focus on.

Certainly, just repeating an invocation to light will not magically make you feel lighter. It requires the conscious choice to *engage* the idea or feeling of lightness, in whatever way works for you. It took a while for this principle to evolve from theory to practice for me, to go from thinking or talking about lightness to actually *feeling* it. In fact, when I was younger and learning about some of the deeper teachings of yoga, I sometimes felt like I was faking it. I read the words myself and then said the words to my students: *"Relax and settle into a state of lightness. Let go of what is burdening you."* But what was really happening? Looking back on it now, years later, it was like a lightbulb had been turned on at the low end of a dimmer switch. I saw something in these teachings, but it started out faint.

One reason I felt like I was faking it as a younger yoga student and teacher was because, like every human, I had a whole set of past experiences and reactions to those experiences which had formed my personality, complete with a basic "filter" through which I saw the world and reacted to it. Again, like most humans, my filter had a particular notch where a little doubting voice resided. The voice might say, *What makes you think just because you say 'let go of your worries' it's anything more than just telling yourself what you want to hear?* Through more study (particularly of the *Yoga Sutra of Patañjali;* see Chapter 5), I came to understand that, according to the yoga tradition, the doubting voice in our minds is, in fact, merely an *aspect* of mind. The mind fluctuates, it wavers and changes, like the weather. What does not change is our inner self, our inner wisdom. That is the voice I learned to listen to. I learned how to recognize my filter and go around it when it was clouding my perception.

Over time and with more practice, the light switch gradually moved from dimmer to brighter. You might think of it as a case of "fake it 'til you make it." And I guess that's true. But there's something important to consider about that catchphrase: It's based in reality. I've said that positive imagery was one of the key tools I used throughout cancer treatment. And that choice was made, in large part, based on what I'd learned about neuroplasticity, the brain's ability to change: Repeated patterns of mental activity actually change the structure and function of the brain. In other words, *we become what we habitually think.*[3]

I was learning something. It was the idea of "banking" my good thoughts and feelings.

Now, it's not like I did this yoga practice for depression and suddenly I was light-hearted and free for the rest of my treatment. But I could sense a shift in the right direction. I was learning something. It was the idea of "banking" my good thoughts and feelings. On days when I felt good and strong and positive, I intentionally imprinted those feelings and sensations on my memory and in my body. Then, on days when I had nothing, no motivation, no energy, I could tap into my bank account and remember what I had stored away. Just knowing those positive feelings were in there somewhere helped me access them, so if I couldn't quite conjure up authentically good vibes, I trusted in the promise that they'd be there another day.

Back on that morning, I sat quietly in meditation, listening to my teacher's recording. He offered a reminder to recognize our ability to choose what we focus on. This was the invitation to use positive imagery, to reinforce an uplifting mindset again on this day. In that moment, with my "filter" turned off, I felt myself making a conscious choice of lightness over heaviness. Here was the actual experience rather than the thinking process. I could see myself gently swatting away tiny doubts about whether this practice had validity. After all, a negative mindset is nothing more than a choice itself. It is no more "right" than a positive mindset. It's just that the positive mindset is exponentially more nourishing.[4]

## HOW YOGA HELPED

I mentioned in Chapter 8 that I've often thought my mom would have appreciated yoga if she'd learned more about it before her death from brain cancer in 2000. I wonder if, as I continued my yoga studies, I might have been able to show her some practices that could have helped when she was feeling the weight of depression. Or even helped her find a new angle of perception in the self-study she was surely doing, perhaps shifting her relationship to the roots of her depression.

But having seen how hard it was for her to get out from under that weight, I wasn't sure about the extent to which yoga could have helped. I tended to see medication as the necessary basis for her treatment, even though I was aware of how difficult it was to find the right dose and combination of meds. A good friend and colleague with extensive experience in yoga for mental health, Kristine Weber,[5] reminded me

that I may not have been giving yoga enough credit. Depending on the physiologic nature of certain types of depression, yoga can be just as effective as medications.[6] Because of yoga's holistic nature—those Five

Aspects—it might be more useful to employ yoga rather than Western medicine as the overarching treatment approach for depression, under which other treatments like medication and cognitive behavior therapy could be added.

I can't know exactly what yoga could have done for my mom, but it certainly might have been an avenue for her to explore, including practices to regulate the nervous system, increase energy, and help reframe perspective. This is what I hope for you, if you experience the "tamped down" feeling of depression as you're going through cancer treatment.

## If your depression is more serious and long-lasting, please seek clinical help from your medical team.

In yoga therapy, we learn that one strategy for dealing with depression is engaging in strong, vigorous exercise to increase energy and lift our spirits. It does this primarily by balancing our autonomic nervous system, which, in turn, affects overall healthier body functioning and a more stable mood. You can do any sort of exercise that's safe for you. For me, especially during cancer treatment, yoga was the ideal exercise because it anchored my mind and offered countless ways to adapt to my changing condition. The first time I did my practice for depression, I was able to go full on, doing all the strong postures and holding them for several breaths. A few months into chemo, though, I slowed everything down, skipped some postures, and decreased the length of my breath. Regardless of how you might need to "calibrate" the intensity of a practice,

the overall intention is to keep your energy moving in an upward direction.

You can see a full-length sample **practice for depression** in Chapter 22. For times when physical exercise is out of the question, the breath exercises and/or meditation on their own can be excellent, even primary, strategies. Vocal chanting is a key feature of this practice. Not only does vocalizing stimulate emotional parts of the brain, but the meaning of the chant itself becomes a focal point, nudging the mind again and again toward the light and away from the heavy. You can chant a line from a song, like "Here Comes the Sun," or make up your own verse, like "A new day shines" or "Morning light, warm and bright." Then believe in your words!

When you don't have time for a full practice, see the simpler breath practice to lift energy, below.

# ALTERNATE-NOSTRIL INHALE

I introduced the *Calming Left Inhale/Right Exhale* exercise in Chapters 2 and 7. In that technique, the combination of inhaling through the left nostril and exhaling through the right had an overall calming effect on the nervous system.

In the *Alternate-Nostril Inhale* technique below, we alternate inhaling through one valved nostril and exhaling through both. Inhaling through one nostril at a time has an overall uplifting and balancing effect on our energy level,[7] making it a very helpful practice for depression symptoms. We can further enhance that energizing effect by gradually increasing the length of the breath and adding a pause after the inhalation.

On the exhalation, we gently valve the glottis (the middle region of the voice box), making a soft hissing sound. It feels like you're "dragging" the breath through your throat. This glottal valve is known in yoga as *ujjayi* ("oo JAI ee"), and we use it often in posture practices and seated breath practices. It helps smooth out and slow down the breath.

*Here are the steps:*

1. Sit tall (see Position A). Relax your shoulders and facial muscles and any tension you feel in your body. Start with **Three Simple Breaths** in and out through the nose.

POSITION A

2. Rest the thumb and ring finger of the right hand just below the bridge of the nose; you'll be **partially blocking, or valving,** both nostrils.

3. Slide the thumb down to fully block the right nostril, and **inhale through the valved left nostril** (see Position B).

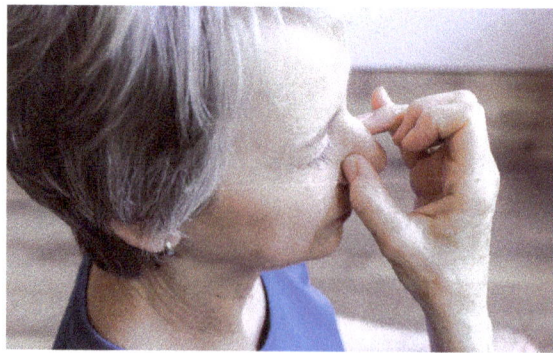

POSITION B

4. Release your hand and **exhale** through both nostrils, gently valving the glottis to make a soft hissing sound; lightly pull in the belly on the exhalation.

5. Now use the ring finger to fully block the left nostril and use the thumb to valve the right, and **inhale through the right nostril** (see Position C).

POSITION C

6. Release your hand and **exhale** through both nostrils, gently valving the glottis to make a soft hissing sound; lightly pull in the belly on the exhalation.

7. Continue the pattern, breathing smoothly and comfortably:

   • Inhale through valved left nostril.

   • Lower your hand and exhale through both nostrils with the *ujjayi* valve.

   • Inhale through valved right nostril.

   • Lower your hand and exhale through both nostrils with the *ujjayi* valve.

8. Gradually lengthen the breath, keeping the length of inhale and exhale equal. Add a pause after each inhalation. During the pause, let the throat remain relaxed. An example pattern might be:

   • Inhale for 6 counts.

   • Pause for 3 counts.

   • Exhale for 6 counts.

   • Eventually you may increase to inhale 8, pause 4, exhale 8. The requirement for increasing the length is that your breath is smooth and comfortable, never forced. If you force your breath, the exercise starts to feel agitating. So let the breath lead the way!

9. Start with a few rounds, working up to 2 minutes, and then 5 minutes.

10. When you finish, take time to notice what you feel. Notice the quality of your breathing, the level of energy you feel, what your mind is doing, your overall emotional state. There is no right or wrong way to feel. The practice is about doing, then noticing from an objective point of view. The more we do this, the more familiar we become with shifting into our calm, balanced, objective center. And this is where we see most clearly.

## A MULTI-PURPOSE TECHNIQUE

The *Alternate-Nostril Inhale* technique is not only for when you're feeling low. It's a wonderful exercise for any time you want to lift your energy in a balanced way.

You may be thinking, *How do we do that—increase energy while also feeling balanced?*

Think of it this way: drinking a cup of coffee stimulates your energy, but it may also create agitation, a "buzzy" feeling.

*Alternate-Nostril Inhale* perks up the body's nervous system without the buzz.

Each inhalation is a mini-boost for the body. By gradually lengthening the inhalation, and holding it in for a pause, we augment its energizing effect. And because we are inhaling alternately through the nostrils, we are giving an equal boost to the right side, which is associated with the "activating" side of our nervous system, and to the left side, which is associated with the "relaxing" side of our nervous system. The result is an increase in energy which is neither over-stimulating nor over-sedating, but rather, balanced.

Try it in the morning to get your day started. Or midday when you feel tired and you may be likely to reach for a stimulant like coffee or soda or sugar. You'll want to avoid this technique before bed or at times when you want to calm down your energy.

## HOW OTHERS CAN HELP

This is important: talk to a loved one or friend if you are feeling symptoms of depression. Just by talking about it, we usually feel lighter, more hopeful. Accept their help—it's something small they can do that will help you in a big way. If your symptoms are serious and/or are lasting longer than a few days, seek professional help. If you don't know who to call, reach out to your oncologist or primary care physician for a referral.

# CHAPTER 12

# ROCKY, DON'T YOU FORGET ABOUT ME

Many months after completing chemotherapy, I was driving home to New Jersey after spending a weekend with Andy in Connecticut. He had moved back to his place once I no longer needed his help on a daily basis. I loved my time alone in the car, especially listening to podcasts. On this day, I listened to one called *Hidden Brain*, a blend of neuroscience and storytelling that explores the unconscious patterns that drive our behavior.[1] That day's episode was about ways people can use sight, both our eyesight and our mind's eye, to meet challenges and find solutions. An example is a marathon runner who sets her vision on a distant street sign, seeing only that object as her goal until she reaches it, passes it, and sets her sights on the next sign, repeating the process all the way to the finish line. Research has shown this technique reduces the perceived exertion in athletes and increases their overall performance. Thinking back, I realized I had used that "sight" strategy throughout chemotherapy. I kept a mental image of each chemo date on my calendar as a goal, and tried to concentrate only on that date rather than on the entire time period. *I just have to reach next Thursday….* Finally, I reached the last Thursday. January 9, 2020. It happened to be the day before my son Michael's 26th birthday, which made it extra special.

Walking out of the chemo suite for the final time that winter afternoon, I headed directly toward the next hurdle: an appointment with a radiation oncologist. I knew from my earliest days of treatment that I needed radiation following surgery and chemo. But I'd definitely filed it in a "cross-that-bridge-when-we-come-to-it" folder in my mind. And now we'd come to it. Dr. M., the radiation oncologist, explained I would need six weeks of radiation, Monday through Friday.

"Really? Six weeks?" I asked. "I was hoping it would be more like four." Somehow, I had convinced myself that the radiation part of the treatment might be negotiable.

Dr. M. smiled. He was probably in his late thirties with a young face. He wore glasses and had a mild manner. "Nope. It's six."

He explained my two options: either a traditional course of "photon" radiation or a national clinical study using a method called "proton" radiation. The primary difference is that a traditional photon beam is more likely to scatter radiation through the overall target area, whereas a proton beam reaches its target and then essentially stops, purportedly causing less damage to surrounding tissue. I'm oversimplifying a complex process, but in the case of a left breast cancer like mine, proton treatment could spare heart and lung tissue from receiving undue radiation, perhaps preventing future complications.

I had just finished three hours of chemo and wasn't prepared to make a decision right then and there. I had questions and wanted to pick the best treatment. To help my decision making, Dr. M. made an appointment for me to see his colleague, Dr. C., who was the lead researcher of the photon/proton study. One of the things I love about integrated cancer centers is their efficiency. Appointments were made for me, so I didn't have to call around, and they usually happened within days. That service is so valuable when you're going through cancer treatment.

Two days later, I drove to Manhattan to meet Dr. C. He turned out to be one of my favorite doctors. He spent half an hour talking with me and listening to my questions. And he was interested in my yoga therapy practice.

He said, "I only have a little experience with yoga but I know it's very helpful. It's good to stay flexible, because radiation causes muscle tissue to contract and get really tight." (At the time, I had no idea how central that issue would become.)

I asked him about photon verses proton treatment.

He gave me a brief history of radiation therapy for breast cancer, in which he'd played a prominent role.

I said, "So you're the head of this big national proton study. You must believe that it has advantages over photon, right?"

"Not exactly. We can't go into research trying to prove the thing we want to see."

He explained that proton therapy had been around for many years and had been used to treat several cancers, including breast cancer. But more evidence was needed to show its efficacy compared to photon radiation for breast cancer.

"Even then, it's nuanced. We might find it's better for specific kinds of breast cancers. So far, we've seen positive outcomes, but the study still has several years to go."

Then, he talked about what is involved in collecting accurate data, the precision required at the delivery level where radiologists and technicians need to follow exact specifications. If those protocols are not followed, data may be unusable. I was reminded of how much time and energy go into a clinical study. It would feel good to contribute to that process, especially since every aspect of my treatment was made possible because someone else had agreed to be part of a prior study.

Finally, he said, "In your case, both photon and proton treatments are going to be highly successful."

Even though I was looking for answers, I appreciated that he wasn't going to try and persuade me one way or another. He was just giving me information. Ultimately, it was my choice.

Once I made my way through the tangle of Manhattan traffic and crossed the George Washington Bridge, I could settle into thinking for the rest of the drive home. I liked the idea of getting proton treatment and sparing the tissue around my heart and lungs. But there were some things to consider:

- Both types of therapy were expected to be highly successful in my case.

- I could join the study and hope I was randomized into the proton group.

- If I didn't want to leave it up to chance, I could choose proton treatment on my own, outside of the study. In that case, I would be under the care of a physician outside of Sloan Kettering, who would be a radiation oncology generalist, rather than a breast cancer specialist.

- My insurance plan would cover the traditional photon treatment, but might not cover the proton study, which could cost up to $5000 out of pocket. (Ultimately, the radiation center and the insurance company were still going back and forth years later. What a crazy system.)

Both photon and proton had pros and cons. I went around and around trying to decide. I realized I needed to identify my priority in order to make the decision. In the end, I decided that the most important factor for me was to stick with the Sloan Kettering team. The only way to get proton treatment under Dr. C.'s care would be to take my chances with randomization into the study. I enrolled and, happily, I ended up in the proton group. My decision was a personal one; it was right for me, but I certainly wouldn't suggest mine was the best choice for everyone. I learned it felt empowering to claim my priority, and then allow that priority to lead the way forward. A sense of agency truly helps when you're dealing with difficult circumstances, like figuring out which sort of radiation will be zapping you five days a week over six weeks.

My first appointment at the proton therapy center was a simulation to set up for the actual treatments. I was given a white waffle-weave robe to keep and wear at each treatment. As is always my experience with one-size-fits-all garments, I was swimming in the robe. Why isn't this taken into consideration when places like hotels or breast imaging centers order their gowns? They only ever have extra-large. Why can't they just order different sizes? Would it kill them to throw in a few extra-smalls? Why should smaller people have to walk around looking like kids dressing up in their mom's bathrobe while taller people look like actual adults? But since I have worked through all my "small" issues in life (*wink, wink*), I just smiled at my reflection in the changing room mirror and headed out to the patient waiting area.

From there, I was shown to a large room with a humming CT scan machine (Computed Tomography uses computers and rotating X-rays to create detailed cross-sectional images of the body). This was to get a baseline image of my heart before the radiation treatments began. Later, after treatment was complete, this image would be compared to a postradiation scan to see if there had been any damage to my heart. The team of four medical technicians were friendly and relaxed. They had me lie down on a hard, skinny table with my left arm stretched up over my head and my head turned to the right. Underneath me was a blue plastic bag filled with a liquid chemical that was nice and warm in contrast to the frigid temperature in the room. The technicians taped the plastic bag to my arms and belly with painter's tape. Over the course of ten minutes the liquid chemical expanded and then hardened, creating a mold that cradled my upper body. I would lie in this mold for all of my radiation treatments so I would be in exactly the same position each time.

Once the mold was created, the technicians shifted me around on the table to line up my body relative to a set of laser beams. They used Sharpie markers to draw a set of four marks on my torso to match up with the lasers. My hips needed an adjustment, and that meant they had to smudge out the marks with rubbing alcohol and draw new marks. After that, they left the room to run a scan. But before the scan started, they came back in to adjust me one more time and redraw the four marks again! Finally, everything was just where they wanted it. The table I was lying on slid under an arched CT scan machine. Only my chest was covered, so it wasn't claustrophobic at all.

I had to lie still for about thirty minutes while all of this was taking place. I relaxed, breathed smoothly, and tried to mentally repeat the chant from my go-to yoga practice (*wisdom, energy, blessings*). But there was so much going on with the four technicians talking, loud fans whirring, and a really good seventies radio station playing above the din of the machines that I just sank into the music. I heard Bill Withers' "Just the Two of Us," Steve Miller's "Fly Like an Eagle," and Stevie Nicks' "Landslide," which always strikes a poignant chord for me, especially the line, *"I'm getting older, too."* So much is said in such a short phrase.

## I stayed focused on breathing to keep myself anchored in the here and now.

Lying there, a captive audience to my thoughts, I felt a bittersweet feeling come over me—the march of time. In an instant, my mind flipped through a dozen or more snapshots, seemingly banal moments. At 13, riding my mustard-yellow bike home from a friend's house, the summer air smelling like sweet freedom. At 19, returning to college after summer break, anticipation and independence captured in the September sunlight glittering through trees on the brick dorm buildings. I let these and other moments course through my mind and my heart. At the same time, I stayed focused on breathing to keep myself anchored in the here and now. It was very helpful for me to be able to recognize the emotions and memories stirred up by that song—the way unremarkable moments on ordinary days are the very stuff of our lives—and to be able to acknowledge and appreciate them, but also let them move on naturally.

Once the scan was complete, we waited for a cardiologist to confirm everything was okay. With that go-ahead, one of the techs gave me a permanent tattoo the size of a pinhead on each of the four Sharpie spots on my torso (*yes, people, I now have tats!*). This meant the spots would not wash off; more insurance that everything would be lined up exactly right for the radiation treatments, which would start three weeks later.

As I was leaving the center that day, a receptionist came out from behind the front desk. She took me by the arm and pointed to a bell mounted on the wall next to the exit. She said, "See that bell there? On your last day of treatment, we have a big celebration. You'll ring that bell three times and we play the theme from *Rocky* over the loudspeakers and you get to take your victory lap!"

I didn't want to rain on her parade, but my immediate thought was, *I won't be doing that.*

Don't get me wrong, I could envision my last day of treatment. I could see the calendar in my mind and imagine that each Friday of my six weeks would be a mini goal reached. I could imagine the joy and relief I'd be feeling on the last Friday. And even though I loved *Rocky* and saw it multiple times in 1976, at this point in my life, I wasn't the bell-ringing, victory lap-taking, make-a-fuss type. I was picturing something more like Judd Nelson at the end of *The Breakfast Club,* walking off as the sun rises, one arm raised in victory, the sound of Simple Minds' "Don't You Forget About Me" swelling to a crescendo—inside my head, not on a loudspeaker. Yeah, that's gonna be my goal.

## HOW YOGA HELPED

When I was lying on the CT scan table, it was difficult for me to focus on my go-to mantra (*wisdom, energy, blessings*) because of all the noise in the room. I decided to just let the noise, in this case, the music that was playing, become my focal point. Sometimes, with old songs I've heard a million times, I catch myself not actually *listening*; it's more like I'm constructing the notes and lyrics from memory a nanosecond ahead of the music on the radio. On this day, I focused with purpose. I turned my attention and my awareness to my ears, hearing the music in the present moment rather than anticipating it. Here's a way you can try it.

# PRESENT MOMENT LISTENING

1. Play a song that you love and have heard many times.

2. Sit down and close your eyes. Take three simple breaths, slowly in and out.

3. Tune your attention to your ears; maybe you can feel or sense the physical outer ears. Maybe you can even sense the inner ears.

4. Let your familiar song flow in through your ears, as if you are "tasting it" or "drinking it in." Let the sound wash over you. Resist singing along in your head. This time just *hear* it. Hear all the instruments. Hear the singer's voice. Connect with the human beings who played and sang on the particular day this song was recorded.

5. This exercise is a meditation of sorts (remember, the basic definition of meditation is holding your attention on one focal point), and as with other meditations, you may find that your mind wanders. You may start singing along or constructing the song in your head. If that happens, just return your attention to your ears, feel them with your awareness, and let the music flow through them again.

Of course, when it comes to old songs, they tend to have the most emotional impact on us. Feelings might come up, like when I heard Stevie Nicks singing, *"I'm getting older, too."*

This is where I relied on an important yoga principle called *vairāgya*, which I mentioned at the end of Chapter 9. *Vairāgya* means "nonattachment." It refers to letting go of our emotional entanglements with the past and the future so that we are not stuck at the mercy of either old feelings or what-if worries. It doesn't mean we should forget past experiences or ignore the future. Rather, *vairāgya* intends that we recognize when memories spark strong emotions, yet we remain balanced. Yoga texts refer to finding a state of *equanimity*, a word that feels sweet and steady to me. If we can remember that emotional states are temporary, like the weather, then we can let the feelings move on through while we remain anchored in the present. Not resisting, but riding it out.

The best anchoring tool, of course, is your breath. You might try it like this:

- If your song brings up strong emotions, turn your attention to your breath. Feel the tip of your nose. Feel the two columns of air flowing into and out of your nostrils. Focus on that physical sensation.

- Acknowledge the feeling. You can even talk to it in your mind: *Hello, wistful feeling of nostalgia. Boy, I loved those days when I was a kid. Go ahead and run your course. I'm just going to breathe and relax.*

- Continue feeling your breath. Let your belly be soft as you breathe. Relax your shoulders, jaw, tongue, forehead.

- Resist the temptation to "feed" the emotion, to replay it. Just watch it as you breathe, feeling your body on the chair, feeling your clothes on your body, feeling yourself to be present here and now.

- When you feel the emotion has run its course, finish by taking three simple breaths, counting them mentally. Feel each inhalation and each exhalation.

- Notice any shift in your emotional state. Notice that you did it: You felt an emotion arise, you acknowledged it, you breathed while it lingered, you *experienced* and *honored* it. And you watched it move on. Maybe you discovered a new realization about it. You have that ability.

Sometimes we want to sink into the comforting feelings that memories conjure. They can be a welcome escape. That's okay, as long as we are aware we're doing it and remain aware that memories are not where we are now.

Sometimes memories spark strong, difficult feelings. As shown in the exercise above, we can use our breath to ride out these waves of emotion. But this can be tough. We have strong instincts to avoid unpleasant feelings. So we often try to get away from them by ignoring them, or overeating, -talking, -shopping, -working, -drinking … you get the picture.

The wisdom of yoga, however, points out that avoiding an unpleasant feeling won't make it disappear; in fact, it can make the feeling stronger. A better choice is learning to feel our feelings while holding our steady seat, practicing *equanimity*. And that's not easy. Which is why it's so valuable to practice this kind of thing along the road of our lives, so when we hit the inevitable rough patches, like cancer or pain or loss, we have a little experience dealing with the rise and fall of emotions.

## HOW OTHERS CAN HELP

Some people do best when they work through emotions on their own. Others do better if they have a loved one, friend, or therapist to talk to. The key is finding your way to see where the emotions come from, so you can see them clearly for what they are and not mistake the tides of emotions for your true, inner self. A wise person described it to me this way: "Who do you want driving the bus of your life? Six-year-old you or present-day you?" When we let the six-year-old take the wheel, we're reacting from past experiences and actually reinforcing them. Better to buckle the six-year-old self into their seat as you take over the driving!

# CHAPTER 13

# LET'S BRIGHT SIDE THIS

Radiation was something I had successfully avoided thinking about since beginning cancer treatment. Up until now, I'd faced everything—surgery, chemotherapy, genetic testing, more surgery—with a pretty good attitude. I had made a conscious decision not to spend time wondering, *How did I get breast cancer?* Or, *Why did I get it?* I had it, that was the fact. I knew the best thing to do was treat it and keep myself as healthy as possible in the process.

But there was one stubborn little thought camped out at the back of my mind: I didn't want to have radiation. I really didn't want to. The chemo was bad enough; somehow I felt my body could fight back, slough off, and recover from that onslaught of drugs.

Radiation was another story. After all, radiation is something to be *avoided*. Radiation causes cancer. The stubborn little ball of denial was very clear: I didn't want more of *that*! But the research supported the combination of treatments my team had consistently advised: surgery, chemo, radiation. The recovery rates with this protocol were very high. Dr. C. had said 97 percent. As much as I didn't want to have radiation, I also knew I was not the person who was

going to forego Western medicine and undergo alternative treatments. I know there are many people who have done things just like that, across lots of areas of life, and had remarkable experiences. But it wasn't me. I realized I had to get my attitude on the right track. I had six weeks of radiation, Monday through Friday, to get through. I absolutely needed to keep up a positive mindset and maintain my strength and stamina.

To make things more complicated, COVID-19 was just beginning to spread in New York and New Jersey. In early March 2020, there were six cases of it in New Jersey. Six weeks later, the state was averaging 3,000–4,000 new cases and 200–350 deaths per day. *Per day.* It was, and still is, hard to wrap our minds around these statistics.

It was during those six weeks of the state's initial stay-at-home order that I went through radiation treatment. I needed a way to manage the uncertainty of entering a medical facility every day as the virus spread unchecked. And a way to manage the usual stressors over radiation, like skin damage, muscle and joint dysfunction, and fatigue. Not to mention the possible future effects of the "cure," like secondary cancers.

To tackle all of those concerns, I used three practices. The first was a breathing exercise I used whenever I felt anxious. The second was a visualization to use while I was on the proton table to help create a sense of cooling, healing energy to oppose the radiation. The third practice was done at home after each treatment to address fatigue and to maintain mobility in my left arm, shoulder, and neck. I didn't always need the first one, but I did the second and third practices every day without fail. You can see the practices at the end of this chapter and Chapter 14.

In those early days of the pandemic when public information was scant, we worked out our own safety strategies, and maybe went overboard—better safe than sorry. To prepare for my daily trip to radiation, I ordered several masks and a box of nitrile gloves. I put these in a tote bag, along with the extra-large waffle-weave robe I'd been issued at my simulation. I also added a canister of Clorox wipes, a travel-sized hand sanitizer, and a tube of skin cream.

Each day, I arrived at ProCure, the treatment center, around 7:00 A.M. I waited in my car for a call saying they were ready for me, since only one patient at a time was admitted during the pandemic. I donned my mask and gloves, which were mandatory at the center, and had my temperature checked at the entrance. From there I went to the changing room where I developed a system that I'm sure would qualify as top-notch obsessive-compulsive. First, I wiped off the chair with a Clorox wipe and set down my tote. Then I removed my coat, shirt, and bra, all of which I held between my knees while I pulled my robe out of the tote and put it on. Then I put my clothes into the tote. Using another Clorox wipe, I punched a code into the keypad on the locker, wiped down the hook inside and hung the tote bag on it. I closed the locker with the wipe still in my hand, opened the dressing room door, and threw away the wipe. Then, for good measure, I held my hand under the hand sanitizer dispenser on the wall and cleaned my gloved hands. Finally, I stood in the patient area rather than sitting on any of the chairs that someone else may have recently sat on (even though I was usually the first patient of the day) and waited to be taken to the proton room.

My routine continued, in reverse, when I returned to the locker and got dressed again. Before getting into the car, I removed my mask and gloves the way I'd learned when I worked at a hospital, and then sanitized the hell out of my hands *again*, as well as the door handle, steering wheel, and gear shift. Back home, I would hang my tote bag in the garage and put my clothes directly into the washing machine upon entering the house. I rotated through a set of four different masks and even four different hats (I had only a light growth of peach fuzz by this time), hanging them on hooks in the garage, giving them several days to air out. And regardless of these measures, I was still fearful all the while that I was carrying the virus home with me each day. These were the early days of the pandemic, when we didn't understand how the virus was transmitted and how to reasonably stay safe. When we wondered how to be around each other without offending anyone by standing either too close or too far away. There was a sense of foreboding everywhere, as if there were no way to avoid the invisible invader.

It was weird to be worried about something other than cancer.
At the same time, the unknowns about the virus seemed
to coalesce into a generalized, existential ball of fear.

Not surprisingly, the first couple weeks of radiation were highly stressful. I would feel the tightness of anxiety in my chest and gut as soon as I pulled into the parking lot at ProCure. I practiced a calming breath technique in my car before entering the building and again as I stood in the patient waiting area. It was weird to be worried about something other than cancer. At the same time, the unknowns about the virus seemed to coalesce into a generalized, existential ball of fear. Was getting this virus inevitable? How were we going to manage our daily lives? What should I do to keep my two children safe, recognizing they were young adults wanting to make their own decisions? And, by the way, what about the accelerating pace of climate change? Was the world actually on the collision course with self-destruction that we've known all along it was on? Things were spiraling out of control, both outside and inside my mind.

I did my best to keep my mindset close to home, just as I was keeping my body safe at home as we navigated the early days of the pandemic. I focused as much as possible on doing my job of staying healthy. And certainly, I engaged in the common coping mechanism of "bright siding." I reflected on the fact that, through much of my treatment so far, I'd needed to avoid people and germs, so by the time the pandemic hit, I was pretty good at staying home. When I look back on it, I feel lucky that I spent those first weeks of the pandemic in a medical setting, where everyone was trained to deal with germs. I was also grateful that the proton center was not a hospital where people would be seeking treatment for the virus. The safety protocols they put in place helped me relax. After the first week or so of feeling awkward wearing a mask and gloves and maintaining physical distance, I began to feel more comfortable and to trust that this routine was going to work.

## HOW YOGA HELPED

For the first couple weeks when I arrived for my radiation appointment, I was pretty nervous. So before going in, I sat in my car and did the breath practice on the following page two to three times. With each round, I gradually increased the length of my breath. My goal was to be able to breathe slowly and smoothly without feeling any tightness in my chest or belly when I was done. Usually, I needed to do it again once I was in the patient waiting area.

I also discovered another pandemic bright side as I was standing there waiting to be called into the treatment room. Having a mask on with no one else around makes it pretty easy to just say a few calming words out loud to yourself! So, I did that too, if needed. I might say, "Jules, you're doing fine. Just keep going." (True confession: I loved wearing a mask at the grocery store so I could narrate my shopping list and sing along to the 80's soundtrack!)

# "SIPPING BREATH" TO CALM ANXIETY (SEE ALSO CHAPTER 8)

*Although it is unlikely, if at any time while you are doing this technique you feel more anxious, light-headed, or dizzy, stop and breathe in any way that comes naturally. You know your own body best, so follow your instincts.*

### Instructions

1. **Inhale 3 little "sips,"** followed by a long exhalation through pursed lips, as if you're playing the flute. Let the sips be slow and smooth, rather than quick and sharp. Notice your belly draws inward when you exhale. On the next set of inhale sips, let your belly expand out again.

2. **Continue for about 5 rounds.** Then, pause and take a few natural breaths with no specific technique.

3. Then, **take 2 sips** to inhale and exhale through pursed lips.

4. **Continue for about 5 rounds.** Then, pause and take a few natural breaths with no specific technique.

5. If you are feeling calmer, shift to **1 smooth inhalation.** Exhale slowly and smoothly, **this time through the nose,** instead of through the pursed lips.

6. After 5 rounds, notice how you feel: your body, your breath, your mind. If you still feel anxious, you can repeat the process.

## HOW OTHERS CAN HELP

If a friend or loved one is with you, have them read these instructions out loud to guide you through the exercise. You could also record yourself or a friend reading the instructions and keep it on your phone so you can access it any time you need it.

# CHAPTER 14

# COOL, COOL, COOL

*Let your Soul stand cool and composed before a million universes.*

WALT WHITMAN

Each morning at the radiation center, I stood in the pandemic-empty patient waiting area until a technician wearing a mask and gloves came to escort me to the treatment room. Along the way, we would pass an alcove where body molds for all the current patients hung on a rolling rack. The molds—a mix of shapes and sizes, some upper body, some lower—were a pale flesh color with permanent folds in the once pliable plastic bag that became frozen in place during our pretreatment simulations. They hung from large hooks at odd angles. It looked like a strange butcher shop.

Once in the treatment room, I was asked to say my name and address, a comforting daily protocol, so there was no chance I was getting someone else's prescription that day. Then, I was helped onto a long table in a giant, room-sized tube. All the serious machinery was housed in a cavernous space above the tube. The proton beam itself came from a huge chamber where hydrogen atoms are separated into electrons and protons. The protons are injected into something called

a cyclotron, which accelerates them (and sounds like something from the *Jetsons*!). Then through a degrader which adjusts their energy. And finally, into a tube which delivers the now-calibrated beam via a gantry, which is a huge scaffolding that rotates 360 degrees around the table. All this amazing technology culminated in a flat screen about the size of a computer monitor on an arm that hovered over me.

My mold was already in place on the table. I settled back, fitting my left arm into its over-the-head position and nestling my head into its right-facing cradle. Two technicians on either side of the table then jockeyed me around, gently pulling here and there on the sheet beneath me, lining up my four pin-point torso tattoos with a set of laser beams. They had a funny little shorthand for communicating across the table. When one tech had her side lined up, she would say, "That's me." Then the other would make any final adjustments and confirm, "That's me."

During the first couple weeks, these were mildly tense moments for me because of the pandemic's physical distancing guidelines. It was impossible for these folks to do their job while keeping six feet away from me. Maybe they were as nervous as I was. Over the course of my six-week treatment, we didn't say too much about the pandemic; we just did what we were there to do. They were such nice people, a rotating team of about six. I was so grateful for their expertise and kind approach. They treated people all day long with serious conditions more dire than mine. I imagine in that role you must figure out a way to give the job the seriousness it requires, as well as to hold onto some lightness. That seemed to be the prevailing approach, and I appreciated it. There was always music playing on loudspeakers in the treatment room, just like on the day I had my simulation. Most days, it was a classic rock station, which suited me perfectly, but some days it was a little more current, some days a little country. The techs told me on my first day that I could request any music I wanted, but I was happy to listen to whatever they had selected.

## This practice was all about building a detailed mental image and the physical sensation of coolness to counter the idea of radiation and heat.

After they lined me up on the table, the technicians told me I would hear a doorbell when they left the treatment area to go into the monitoring room, but that they could hear me clearly if I needed anything. At that point, the proton screen would rotate into place, alternating between two positions every other day: either directly over my left breast or angled over my armpit where the lymph nodes were removed. I could hear the machinery whooshing and whirring above the giant tube. But I would already have my eyes closed by this time. I was settling into my "Cool, Cool, Cool Practice." This practice was all about building a detailed mental image and the physical sensation of coolness to counter the idea of radiation and heat.

That might sound strange. I didn't actually think I was going to decrease the dosage of the radiation with my mind or anything like that. In fact, I wouldn't have wanted to do that. But I also didn't want to lay there and focus directly on the radiation. If I started to think about that intense beam penetrating into my body, I knew I might become anxious and go into a fight-or-flight state. That would mean my body was compromised at the very moment it needed to be as strong as possible. In fact, I'd read that some people take anti-anxiety medication right before treatment, which is one way to ward off the stress state. Given how short the treatment time was, I didn't think I would need that. Instead, I wanted to flood my mind with good thoughts, to keep myself in the opposite of fight-or-flight, in the rest-and-digest state. I wanted to let the giant proton machine do its job, and I would do mine, which I saw as keeping things cool.

For some reason, as I was figuring out what I wanted my visualization to be, images of dolphins kept coming into my mind. I'm fascinated with dolphins, like many people are, and have treasured the few times I've seen them from a beach or a boat. I love watching films about them. To me they have a special bearing or demeanor that speaks to my heart. I can't explain it in words. When I see them swimming so swiftly and leaping out of the water, I feel such joy. Perhaps because they seem so joyful themselves. So I decided to go with it. My visualization would be about cooling water and dolphins.

I saw myself on a beach, wading into crystal clear, blue water. I concentrated on feeling the sensation of water touching my skin. I conjured the cool temperature. Occasionally, I would mentally repeat, *cool, cool, cool.* Then a few dolphins would swim over to me. They were ambassadors of a sort, safeguarding and encouraging me to swim freely in the healing waters. And I totally needed their protection, because I am not a strong swimmer! So, conveniently, in my visualization, the dolphins let me hold onto their fins. I felt the feeling of being swept along through the water. Then we might come to a stop to just float and bob. I would imagine the feeling you get when you are submerged, feeling the line of the water right up to my chin so that the whole area of my body that was being radiated was being cooled off, "under water." The dolphins and I communicated magically, and I imagined them reassuring me and inviting me to be free, to be like them. Of course, I know that in the real world dolphins have the same problems that all animals have—finding food and fending off predators. But beyond the bare necessities, I tapped into their natural selves, just being in the world.

No matter what was going on outside my closed eyelids, I tried to stay in this visualization. Some days I would hear unusual noises above me, or the technicians' voices from the monitor room. Some days

the music might be a little distracting. If I felt myself being pulled outward, I'd pause and take three smooth breaths and then refocus on my visualization.

Sometimes another animal would appear in my mind—a bald eagle. This was certainly because I had once seen both a bald eagle *and* a group of dolphins on a whale-watching tour (although we didn't see any whales!). The eagle was perched high on top of a tree along the shore line in Cape May, his stately white head feathers visible all the way from the boat. I have a special affinity to birds of prey as well as to dolphins, so this seemed like a natural addition to my visualization. Of course, I suspended the real-world reality of what a human-eagle interaction would be like, just as I did with the dolphins! In my version, the bird might take me on a flight, letting me ride on his back, feeling the rush of cool air drying the water on my skin. Then the eagle would take me back to the water where the dolphins waited, and, again, I would feel the sensation of submerging into water. And I would encourage the feeling by saying to myself, *cool, cool, cool.*

About this time, I would hear the proton screen retracting. The treatment was over. No more than five minutes had passed, and only ninety seconds of that was the actual radiation. The technicians came back to the table, helped me up, and off I went.

This was the routine for thirty treatments, over and over. It was definitely like Groundhog Day. And the pandemic added its own special flavor to the experience. Waiting in my car to be called in, entering the building one patient at a time, stuck behind a mask, keeping a wide berth from others. The whole thing was pretty solitary. I thought back to my first day at ProCure, when the receptionist told me about their last-day ritual of running out of the building, both fists pumping the air Rocky-style with the theme music playing along. I'd never wanted that fanfare to begin with, so on my final day, I simply walked out of the building. About halfway to my car I said out loud, into my mask, "I'm done!" It felt glorious. And I didn't mind that I was alone in that moment. I'd done this part of the journey on my own, and it felt sweet. The morning sun was just coming out from behind a cloud, reflecting off the wet surface of the nearly-empty parking lot. Although I wasn't going to go so far as to fist pump the air like Judd Nelson in *The Breakfast Club,* in my head I clearly heard: *Don't you forget about me.*

## HOW YOGA HELPED

The "Cool, Cool, Cool Practice" was the visualization practice I used while on the proton table. The intention was to create a sense of cooling, healing energy to counter thoughts of heat and radiation. A visualization practice works best when we tap into as many of our senses as possible—hearing, seeing, smelling, touching, and tasting. It takes focus to stay with the visualization and to keep from veering off into stream of consciousness, but once you do it a few times, it gets easier and easier to "set up" the scene in your mind. It's like telling yourself a story. Mine appears on the following page.

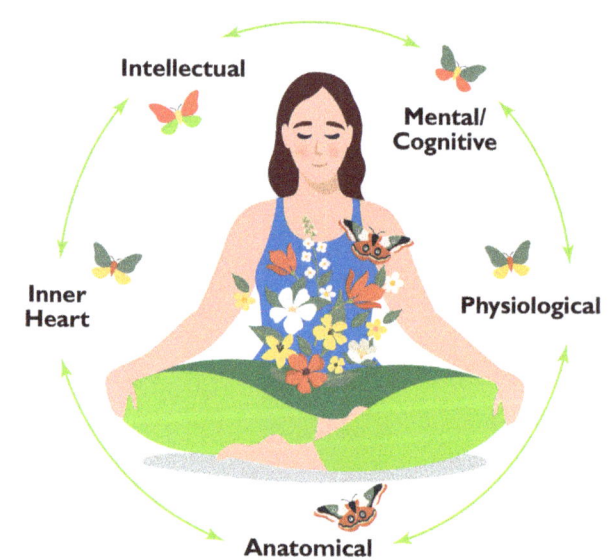

# COOL, COOL, COOL PRACTICE

1. First, I take three simple breaths, slowly, in and out.

2. Then, I picture myself on a beach. I hear a few birds calling. I smell the scent of salt water. I feel the warm sun on my head. Wading into the clear, blue water, I imagine feeling the sensation of cool water, first on my feet, then my legs, my hips, my trunk, my arms, and neck.

3. I spend a moment conjuring what it feels like to be submerged in water, feeling my body in the water and my head out of the water. I feel the line of water right under my chin.

4. Mentally I repeat, *cool, cool, cool.*

5. I imagine several dolphins approaching, gently circling around me, speaking in their dolphin language. I understand that they are saying everything is fine and they'll take good care of me in the water. One of them swims right next to me so I can take hold of his fin. It feels smooth to the touch. Then we began to accelerate through the water. I let go of fear and trust the dolphins. I conjure the feeling of the cool water splashing as we swim on and on.

6. Mentally I repeat, *cool, cool, cool.*

7. On some days, I see my bald eagle friend on a distant tree top. He takes flight and soars with his incredible wing span to where the dolphins and I are floating. He invites me to climb on board and hold onto his strong neck. I feel the tremulous moment when the *whoosh* of his wings lifts us

up and we soar over the water. I feel the air cooling my skin as we fly.

8. Mentally, I repeat, *cool, cool, cool.*

9. When I hear the proton screen retracting, the eagle returns me to the water, and I swim with the dolphins back near the shore. I stay submerged in the water for another moment, letting it cool and heal my skin and all the tissues beneath the skin.

### This is what it means to use our own natural abilities to aid our healing.

I realize that a visualization practice like this isn't for everyone. When I worked as part of a hospital team delivering an outpatient program for cardiac patients, many of the participants were skeptical about visualization, which I was charged with teaching them. They felt it was "not real" or it was just "thinking something because you want to think it." But a lot of research backs up the fact that where our mind goes, our body follows.[1,2,3,4] If we think positive thoughts, our blood pressure, heart rate, and other indicators of homeostasis shift into a positive setting. This is what it means to use our own natural abilities to aid our healing. I was recently watching a reboot of the sitcom *One Day at a Time*. Rita Moreno plays a feisty, seventy-something grandmother, mother, and all-around diva. Another character in the scene, who is a worrier, poses the question, "But what if you *do* get sick?" Rita Moreno looks at him confidently and says, "Then I will cure it *with my mind*!" I laughed and knew that she was absolutely on the right track.

### What's with all the TV references?

By now, I've mentioned so many television shows, especially sitcoms, that you know they were a big part of my healing journey. So, it may come as no surprise that the name of this practice, "Cool, Cool, Cool," was inspired by a sitcom. In *Brooklyn Nine-Nine,* Andy Samberg often tries to hide his character's nervousness by repeating the word "cool" in rapid succession. You think he's surely about to stop, but he keeps going. *And going!* It cracked me up, so I thought of that when I put this practice together.

## HOW OTHERS CAN HELP

If you're having trouble coming up with a visualization, maybe there's someone in your life who can help. Sometimes it makes it easier if another person collaborates with us on something new. You can both dive into it together. Then you or your friend could record the visualization so you can listen to it whenever you need it.

# CHAPTER 15

# APPLY AND REAPPLY

The thing you often hear about radiation is that it is so much easier to go through than chemotherapy. Mostly that's true. People pop in for their radiation treatment in the morning and then head off to a full day of work (although some people do that on chemo, as well). That's because radiation targets localized tissues, rather than being injected into your blood stream, which affects your body's entire physiological system. But radiation comes with its own set of challenges. And they all seem to set in around two weeks into the treatment, slowly building from there.

The most immediate symptom is skin damage. A couple of my yoga students who'd been through radiation told me to moisturize right after the treatment, before driving home. I appreciated that advice. It led me to do some research, so I had three different creams ready to go when I started proton therapy. I'd read about one called Vicco-brand turmeric cream in a book by another person going through radiation, and since I knew that turmeric has anti-inflammatory properties, I decided to try it. Immediately after each treatment, before putting my clothes back on, I applied Vicco all over the left side of my neck, chest,

and armpit. I slathered that stuff on. I fully admit that when this cream first arrived in the mail and I tested it on the back of my hand, I thought, *yuck*. It absorbed easily and it wasn't greasy, but I wasn't sure I could tolerate the lingering turmeric odor or the fact that it would turn my clothes orange. Sure enough, the odor and the color meant nothing once the radiation treatments were actually happening. All I could think about was soothing the bright red skin I saw in the changing room mirror.

At home, I applied another moisturizer every two hours, which my radiation nurse, Elyse, had advised. This one was called Miaderm and was formulated specifically for radiated skin. A friend of a friend had also sworn by it. It was light and absorbent with a pleasant odor. Finally, Elyse had also advised that I alternate the Miaderm, which was available over the counter, with a prescription ointment. This one was thick and took a long time to be absorbed, so it was good to apply right before bed when it would have several hours to sink in. I followed this apply-and-reapply routine religiously every day, even in the beginning when there was no real visible effect from the radiation. For the first two weeks, I thought I had it made. *I'm killing it with my moisturizing regimen. My skin is going to be just fine!* Fast forward to the start of week three, and suddenly my skin started to look red and irritated. I kept on applying.

All of these moisturizers took a toll on my clothes, so I just sacrificed a few shirts to the cause. I wore the same four or five soft cotton shirts over and over. After my final treatment, I thanked them for their service and tossed them! Throughout treatment, some people wear a sports bra for compression because it offers increased circulation, but I was much more comfortable wearing no bra. It was just me at home, and I was fortunate enough not to have to go to work at this time (the pandemic would have kept me home anyway). So, I could easily unbutton and fold open my shirt at the neck, allowing most of the radiated skin to get fresh air, which is great for healing. One of my yoga students said, "Just walk around the house with no shirt on!" Maybe if it hadn't been mid-March and still quite chilly, I would have taken her advice!

By the fourth or fifth week, I understood what she was talking about. My skin started to burn and peel. It actually hurt to have anything, even soft flannel, touch some of the worst spots along the collarbone where the skin is quite thin. At this point, my doctor added a stronger prescription, which helped a lot. I was very thankful to my radiation oncology team for staying so in touch with me and encouraging me to really let them know what my skin looked like and how it felt, because that extra prescription made a big difference.

Still, I was unrealistic about how soon my skin would completely heal. I had kept my mind's eye on the final day of treatment as the starting point for recovery. But somehow, I must have forgotten, or blocked out, that the most visible external effects of radiation continue to worsen for up to two weeks after treatment ends. Thankfully, after those two weeks were over, my skin made a quick recovery. However, I came to learn that, as vastly improved as things looked, the skin would be damaged at some level for a long time, maybe forever. Even 18 months later, I was amazed to see how red my neck would become just from the heat of a shower.

Years after radiation, I continue to apply moisturizer every day. And I absolutely never let that part of my body become exposed to the sun. I faithfully apply sunblock and wear a broad-brimmed hat. And I still use both Miaderm and an all-natural herbal salve on the surgery scars, Healing Salve from Lancasterfarmacy.com.

Watching my skin heal was a really important phase of treatment for me. It was a visible, undeniable reminder of what the body is capable of. If things were healing like that on the outside, certainly healing was also happening beneath the skin. In fact, most of our healing takes place inside the body, within organs and tissues. So, we need to hold on to the faith that it's happening even when we can't see it.

## HOW YOGA HELPED

One way to keep the faith that healing is happening is through discipline, sticking with the program now to ensure a better outcome later.

In yoga, we can relate discipline to a concept called *tapas.* The root of the word *tapas* means "heat," or "cook." In the context of discipline, *tapas* suggests the heat or inner fire that comes when we work at something that challenges us. All of the practices I've talked about so far require *tapas,* an intentional "sticking to it" in order to see some sort of transformation.

Yoga teaches many lessons about discipline. The first and most fundamental one is about disciplining the mind. The ultimate purpose is to let all the fluctuations of the mind settle down so we may feel connected to our quiet, true, inner nature. Healing occurs best in that state.

We learn that one good way to discipline the mind is by disciplining the body and the breath, which we can do through yoga postures and breath techniques. We practice with discipline and observe changes on

the gross level to help us move toward transformation at a more subtle level. Just as I layered on those moisturizers every two hours, knowing they were encouraging healing on the outside, I kept at my daily routine of yoga practice, knowing that it was healing me deep within, as well.

## HOW OTHERS CAN HELP

You could have a friend, or several, agree to do some sort of practice with you each day. It could be yoga and breathing exercises, meditating, chanting, walking. You could meet in person or virtually. Or just exchange a quick picture showing yourselves doing your practice that day.

# CHAPTER 16

# RECOVERY MARATHON

*Always concentrate on how far you've come,*
*rather than how far you have left to go.*

UNKNOWN

loved having the first appointment of the day at Pro-Cure, because it meant I was back home by 8:30 A.M. to begin my yoga practice. It was a refuge for me during those weeks. Spring was coming, and it felt wonderful to have the windows open. I could smell fresh air and see bright green buds on the trees outside my bedroom as I moved through my routine.

During the six months from surgery through chemotherapy, I used my go-to yoga practice with the theme of *wisdom, energy, and blessings*. I had adapted it along the way to address specific symptoms like nausea, constipation, fatigue, depression, and anxiety. When I started radiation, I needed to consider what I would need from my yoga practice during that six-week phase of treatment. Beyond the obvious skin damage, the most pronounced effects of radiation would be fatigue and excessive muscle constriction. I knew there would be emotional effects, as well.

I designed a new practice, using several yoga tools to address multiple symptoms: yoga postures to target neck, chest, shoulder, and arm muscles; breath techniques to increase energy, improve sleep, calm pandemic anxieties, and keep my internal system cool, and finally, chanting to focus healing thoughts on the specific parts of my body receiving radiation.

I did my "Radiation Practice" every morning after returning home from ProCure. The effects of radiation are cumulative, making it crucial to try and stay ahead of them, if possible. For the first two weeks, my body felt "normal." I had full range of motion in my neck, shoulder, and arm. *This will be easy,* I thought. *Obviously, I've figured out how to prevent the tightness and fatigue I've heard so much about.* (Picture me brushing off my shoulders, saying, *I got this.*)

About two weeks into treatment, I started to notice a general feeling of tiredness, a lack of "oomph" as my Nana Weinsheimer would have said. It wasn't as crushing as the fatigue I experienced during chemotherapy, but it was there. I countered it in the same way I had before: by keeping up with whatever exercise I could manage, which was significantly more than during chemo, and by taking it easy when necessary. It was a balancing act.

Soon, I also began to feel tightness when I stretched my left arm overhead. It pulled on the left side of my chest and neck. Small, hard knots of scar tissue under my arm and just below my breast began to bother me. I assumed things would loosen up after radiation ended. But my range of motion continued to decrease after the last treatment, rather than increase. Everything felt more constricted and painful, with faint tingling where the tight muscles in my neck were compressing nerves and where tight connective tissue tugged my breast bone out of place. I would catch myself unconsciously holding my left shoulder up and forward, which only added to the discomfort. My radiation oncology nurse, Elyse, called to see how I was doing. She asked if I needed physical therapy. We were only a couple months into the pandemic at the time, so I was avoiding all nonessential contact with the outside world. I told her I would keep working at it on my own.

I kept stretching and using gentle self-massage every day to try and loosen things up. During the year before my cancer diagnosis, I had completed a massage therapy training, so I understood the anatomy involved in my muscle and nerve pain and knew that scar tissue could be softened over time. At this point I was using very gentle massage, sensing that I didn't want to add to the trauma all of this tissue had

been through. I would soon learn that soft and gentle wasn't the best approach.

In July 2020, I went for my first follow-up appointment with my oncologist, Dr. A., since finishing chemo in January. It was three months after radiation was completed.

"How is everything feeling?" Dr. A. asked as she began her exam.

"Really tight and painful," I said.

"You have to get in there and work through all that constriction," she said, digging her fingers deeply into my breast and armpit area.

"Ouch," I said. I made a face like a "surprised" emoji. She was finding spots I didn't even know were painful until she touched them.

"Yeah, I know, it hurts," she said. "But don't be afraid to really get in there and move the tissue. And it's going to be like this for a long time. It's like Groundhog Day. You think you've loosened it up and the next day when you wake up it's right back where you started."

That offhand comment turned out to be one of the most important things Dr. A. ever said to me. I left her office with a new perspective. This was a marathon, and I had no idea how long the course was or where I currently stood. Even as I sat at my computer later that day, assembling the notes that eventually turned into this chapter, I didn't imagine that I would still be working on my physical recovery for years to come.

## HOW YOGA HELPED

Back at the beginning of this book, I introduced my go-to yoga practice. Once my radiation treatments began, I created a new daily practice to address my changing needs after asking myself some questions.

## WHAT DO I NEED? WHAT TOOLS WILL I USE?

- **Anatomical aspect:** Ease tightness in neck, chest, shoulder, arm. **Tools:** yoga postures

- **Physiological aspect:** Increase energy, stave off fatigue; good night's sleep; calm anxiety about COVID-19; keep inner systems cool in response to the heat of radiation. **Tools:** breath techniques

- **Cognitive, inner heart aspects:** Bring cooling, healing thoughts and attention to the parts of the body being affected by radiation. **Tools:** chanting, meditation

To pull it all together, this time around, I used a yoga theme known as the *Cakra* Model (pronounced *chuk*-ra, not *shock*-ra—there's my inner grammarian peeking out!) to weave all the tools into a logical practice.

The word *cakra* can be translated as *spinning wheel.* It refers to areas along the central axis of the body which are said to "spin" with animating energy. This energy is known as *prāṇa.* It's akin to *chi* from the Chinese traditions. *Cakras* are not exact locations, nor are they physical structures. They are a symbol system for, or a way of describing, the movement of energy and its effect on our multidimensional nature (see Resources at end of book for more on the *cakra* system).

The *Cakra* Model can get pretty complex. But yoga only helps us if we find a way to make it accessible and relevant to our lives. I've been lucky enough to study for many years with a knowledgeable and insightful teacher, Gary Kraftsow. From him, I learned how to sort through the complexity of the *Cakra* Model and distill it down to the essence of what I needed. My *cakra* practice, therefore, focused on the two areas of the body that would be targeted by the proton beam:

- **The heart** *cakra*: This area is associated with, among other things, **the element of air.** I used that association to conjure the idea of a "light and airy touch," which was how I wanted to think of the radiation touching my body.

- **The throat** *cakra*: This area is associated with, among other things, **the element of space.** I used that association to conjure the idea of "open spaciousness," which was how I wanted my muscle and connective tissues to remain, to counter the tightening, constricting effects of the radiation.

I've provided a simple example of a more general *cakra* practice in Chapter 22 that you can modify to suit your needs.

## HOW OTHERS CAN HELP

You may want to seek out a yoga therapist to help you with a postradiation practice, or a physical therapist to get you started on mobilizing the areas of the body that have gotten tight after radiation. As you'll see in upcoming chapters, I kept looking for help, and I encourage you to do the same!

# CHAPTER 17

# I'LL HAVE THE CANCER, WITH A SIDE OF EFFECTS

Just try to relax, Julie."

That instruction came from Matt. He was a physical therapist I sought out in late 2020, several months after my final radiation treatment.

"You gotta be kidding me," was my response.

Matt's thumb kept pressing deeper and deeper into the pectoralis muscle connecting my chest and upper arm. That muscle looked and felt like a steel cable. It was ropey and hard. Surgery and radiation cause damage, from the external skin down through the layers of connective tissue called fascia, which surround and interpenetrate every muscle. In order to repair itself, the body creates thick, fibrous bands of scar tissue out of that fascia. Smoothing out those internal scars can be uncomfortable, to say the least.

"No pain, no gain," was Matt's reply.

This was part of a long journey to try and restore health to my body after the cancer treatments. In addition to tight muscles and scar tissue, I felt achy and fatigued. I had hot flashes and interrupted sleep. My mood was flat and so was my sex drive. Many of these symptoms were caused by the estrogen-suppressing medication I needed to take for at least ten years to prevent a cancer recurrence. There was a lot of posttreatment crap to sort out. I was still running the recovery marathon.

I turned to my doctors and other practitioners for help with several of the medication-induced side effects. I started with the hot flashes. They were having a cumulatively negative effect on my nervous system. Just before a hot flash would start, I felt a sudden sense of dread. Having the hot flash itself didn't make me feel anxious. Instead, it was like an inner warning system was being activated, signaling, *Something distressing is happening and I don't know what it is.* Soon that dread morphed into agitation and my brain started looking around for what was wrong, while my body heated up and I was sweating and desperately gulping ice water. I'd had these hot flashes for ten years prior to starting the estrogen-suppressing medication, and my body was exhausted by the relentless cycle of fight-or-flight that occurred around the clock. Even with the wonderful yoga tools at my disposal, I realized my adrenal system was seriously overtaxed. I felt an underlying tiredness and tension most of the time.

If you're an optimist, like I am, it often takes a while to realize that you've been feeling crappy for a long time!

So, about a year after my cancer treatments, I asked my general practitioner to prescribe a low dose of an anti-depressant, a selective serotonin reuptake inhibitor (SSRI). It was just enough to dampen that dread and the full fight-or-flight state every time I had a hot flash. The flashes still occur, but my body handles them a bit more easily. (Interestingly, when talking to my doctor, a late 30's male, he was scrolling through a list of medications for hot flashes and eventually said, "You're right! SSRIs are on the list. I never knew that before." I explained that many women experience this precursor of dread before a hot flash, while others have nausea signaling an oncoming flash. He said, "You really taught me something today." I told him, "Listen to your women patients. They know their bodies!" He accepted that advice graciously. It was a nice moment with him.)

I thought my yoga practice and knowledge of the body would get me back to full range of motion and out of pain quickly, but that just wasn't the case. Months after treatment I still had trouble with simple activities. I couldn't pull a shirt over my head without pain, couldn't look over my shoulder while driving without turning my whole torso. I needed help.

I sought out several different approaches, including physical therapy, myofascial release, massage, Reiki, integrated manual therapy. There were moments along the way when I felt tired and irritated that I still had to work on all these issues. I seemed to be in a constant state of inner debate.

*I want to be done with cancer already!*

*But I'm never going to be fully done with cancer.*

*And if I stop working on my recovery, I'll be stuck feeling the way I feel at this moment, which is not good enough.*

As long as I continued to have symptoms, I continued to try and reduce them. I am sure there were people in my life who wondered why I was doing all of this. Possibly some of them couldn't keep up with all the different therapists I was seeing. Regardless, I had full support from my sister, my kids, close friends, and, of course, Andy. No matter how many times I told him that I had an appointment with another practitioner, he encouraged me.

"That's wonderful, honey. What have you got to lose? You'll never know if you don't try."

Okay, maybe Andy relies on cliché at times, but he is completely authentic in his belief in self-guided living. If you want to see a change, make a change. If it doesn't work, try something else. He has done that so often for his own health. When traditional physicians balked at his nonconventional ideas about treating his constellation of thyroid, kidney, and adrenal conditions, he kept looking. Finally, he found doctors who saw him as an individual. They supported his willingness to explore different medicines and dosages, even if it meant feeling "pretty crappy," as he put it, until the right balance was found. I definitely had a supportive partner as I chugged along, finding my way back to restored health.

Not everyone needs to see the same kinds of therapists I saw. There are many wonderful resources available to cancer patients during recovery, and many ways of approaching this part of the journey. The most important factor in the process is *you*. I encourage you to search and explore until you find the unique blend of therapies that help to solve the complexity of leftover issues that you are personally dealing with.

## HOW YOGA HELPED

Over months and then years of posttreatment rehab, I turned to my old friend, *vairāgya*, or "nonattachment." I mentioned it in Chapters 9 and 12, as well. It involves letting go, releasing memories of the past and expectations of the future that are not serving you. Instead, it encourages remaining grounded in the present, meeting a situation as if for the first time, each time. I certainly referred to this notion a lot in earlier chapters as I was going through some of the scary stuff, like surgery and chemo.

After the big treatments were over, *vairāgya* translated into letting go of striving to be "back to the way I was" and, instead, to embrace the daily experience of "who I am." It was time for me to directly confront one of the most profound messages that we as yoga therapists offer to our clients: *You are not your condition.*

It was conscious, deliberate work that I carried out with each treatment appointment I went to, holding the intention to be sincerely present at that visit, to keep my head in that moment. Not to link every appointment sequentially to the next, not to expect a linear progression back to my "old self." And most importantly, not to equate my condition, whatever it may be, to my inner self.

Now, if you've stuck with this book all the way through to this point, I consider you a friend, and my friend, I will always be honest with you. Was I *really* sincerely present in every moment at every appointment and did I *always* relinquish all attachment to the outcome of every rehab session?

Of course not.

You know me better than that by now. I'm an earth-bound human, trying to do my best. Like you are. I absolutely got caught up in fretting. Andy was my usual sounding board.

"It's so frustrating. Some of those really tender spots along the breastbone had gotten better. Now they hurt again. I can't figure out what I'm doing wrong and what I should be doing instead."

Luckily for Andy, he often doesn't need to answer, because I just fill in his side of the conversation.

"I know, I know. This isn't a straight line to recovery. It takes a long time to heal, and the whole body is affected, so it isn't about releasing one sore spot and—*poof!*—I'm better. It's about patience and faith in the process."

Cue Andy nodding his head up and down.

If I keep grasping for some other feeling, I will look back and
realize I missed days or months, maybe even years of my life.

I am so grateful for what I've learned from studying yoga. Knowing about *vairāgya* gives me the insight and encouragement to continue living in this moment, to accept what's happening now. It keeps me from obsessing over minute details, like those specific tender spots on the chest muscle, and helps me recognize that the way I feel today is just that—the way I feel today. I don't know how I will feel tomorrow. If I keep grasping for some other feeling, I will look back and realize I missed days or months, maybe even years of my life. Happily, when I employed *vairāgya*, I was able to be much calmer and more accepting of my evolving journey. Which is just the same for any one of us living this life, whether we have cancer or not.

## HOW OTHERS CAN HELP

Sometimes we need others to be a mirror, to reflect back what we are saying, how we are acting. If you find yourself "spinning your wheels" about aspects of your recovery, perhaps ask a trusted loved one or friend to help you look honestly at your actions. Just seeing our own behavior and acknowledging it can be freeing, and often pretty humorous!

# CHAPTER 18

# STRETCHED TO THE LIMIT

*"A mind that is stretched by a new experience*
*can never go back to its old dimensions."*

OLIVER WENDELL HOLMES, JR.

The physical therapy approach that Matt used—deep pressure—can eventually ease the tightness in a muscle which has become "fibrotic" or intensely constricted. But, for me, it was so uncomfortable that instead of my brain sending a signal to relax the muscle, it was telling my body to tense up even more. It felt like no amount of calm yoga breathing or conscious relaxation would work. It hurt like hell. I thanked Matt and moved on.

My next stop took me back to the cancer center where I saw my doctors and had gone through chemo. There, I began seeing Debra, an excellent physical therapist who saw only post-cancer patients like me. You may be asking, "Why didn't you just go there in the first place?" That's a great question, and I don't have a good answer other than that I had worked with Matt several years earlier, so I tried him first. The lesson I learned: Don't be afraid to try something. If it doesn't work, you can always try something new. And don't be afraid to change if a certain treatment just doesn't feel right.

Debra's approach to the physical therapy was kinder and gentler. She never forced uncomfortable manual manipulation. Instead, she eased in slowly, patiently waiting for the tissue to soften so it was more willing to release and stretch. I felt like she was a true partner in my progress. She listened to my feedback and adapted the therapy to my needs. When I explained that one of her exercises was causing back pain, she said, "Let's change it up—we want to solve problems, not cause new ones!" She experimented until we found a way to "customize" the exercise for my body. That's exactly what I do with my yoga therapy clients, and I appreciated finding the same mindset in Debra. Being willing to let go of a "prescription" for recovery is a wonderful asset to our body's own natural course of healing.

Debra was also interested in my yoga practice. I was glad she asked me to demonstrate the postures I was using, because often people have a blanket assumption that all yoga is good for you. But she wanted to see exactly what I was doing to make sure it was helping and not hurting my progress. She agreed with every posture and encouraged me to keep at it. I was glad to have that reinforcement, because I hadn't seen much change in my condition so far.

"Keep working on it," she said. "Most people don't realize how important it is to keep at it. They expect to come to PT once a week for a while and then they're cured. I tell them, 'You have to work on this consistently for a long time, longer than you think.'"

I did the exercises faithfully at home, although they were uncomfortable and even painful at first. Every night when my daughter Emma and I met in the family room to watch whatever reality show we were pandemic-binging at the time, I would pull out my worksheet from Debra and get down on the floor to do my reps. One night after several weeks, I noticed something.

"Look at how much farther I can stretch my arm!"

Curled up on the sofa, Emma said, "Nice work there, little lady." (In fact, Emma is several inches taller than me, so the description fits!)

It felt so good to realize I was affecting this change in my body. And there was still a long way to go.

## HOW YOGA HELPED

When I brought home the worksheets from Debra, I did for myself what I've done for many of my yoga therapy clients who come to me after seeing a physical therapist. I adapted my physical therapy (PT) exercises to a yoga approach: sequencing them in the best order for my body, and specifically indicating inhalation and exhalation in each exercise. This detail greatly increases the precision of the movement while also relaxing the autonomic nervous system, and therefore, the body and mind.

At the same time I was doing the PT exercises, I kept up with my regular morning yoga practice. Like an anchor, that practice was still helping with my original goals of *wisdom, energy, and blessings,* those three key components I'd identified as essential way back when my cancer treatments began. My sessions with Debra reinforced my knowledge/wisdom. The PT and yoga exercises increased my energy. And the consistency of my yoga practice fostered a sense of feeling blessed, on both a small

and a grand scale. Eventually, my yoga practice just absorbed my PT exercises. They remain part of a repertoire that I pull from every day to maintain mobility and strength in my arm, shoulder and chest. I'm grateful to Debra for shepherding me through that early rehab period.

## HOW OTHERS CAN HELP

I highly recommend getting to a physical therapist experienced with post-cancer surgery as soon as you can after surgery. I only waited because of the pandemic, and I wish I hadn't. Establish those good movement habits early on, and then stick with them.

# CHAPTER 19

# CATCH AND RELEASE

*"Your job is to go play and have fun."*

David Crewdson

I ended up going to only five physical therapy sessions with Debra, because I wanted to limit my COVID exposure at the center where she treated other patients all day. But she'd given me a lot of information and instruction. Over the next few months, I made progress, but I still didn't have the level of mobility I was willing to live with for the rest of my life. My shoulder and neck were tight and uncomfortable most of the time. I felt tugging around my ribs when I raised my arm. And there was a nagging pain between my left shoulder blade and my spine.

I started thinking about other cancer patients, people who had not had the advantage of studying the body as I had. I wondered if perhaps many people just accepted a certain level of rehabilitation and left it at that. I thought back and realized that I'd had a few clients like that in my yoga therapy practice. Women who came to see me for an issue like depression or back pain, and who had limited range of motion in their arm or shoulder.

They'd say something like, "Oh yeah, that arm won't stretch any further."

Or worse, they'd apologize for it. "Sorry, it won't straighten out all the way."

I realize now I hadn't taken my assessment far enough in order to link their history of breast cancer with their shoulder restriction. I hadn't seen with "x-ray" eyes, as one of my yoga teachers, Mary, used to say. I didn't see inside to understand that the tightness in their shoulder, most likely from radiation or surgery, extended via the fascial system of connective tissue throughout their whole body and was still there, even though the cancer treatment had happened years prior.

Now I could feel those fascial connections for myself. Fascia is an intricate body system, far more complex than the scope of this book, but as a simplified illustration, imagine a knitted sweater. A "pull" in one of the threads can cause nearby threads to twist or distort. If you keep pulling that thread, the distortion extends farther and farther because the yarn is one continuous material. If you darn those threads to repair the hole, you end up with a "lumpy" line of yarn and a section where the sweater doesn't have the same "spring" as the rest of the garment.

That's basically how fascia works. When there is any sort of injury or trauma, fibers of connective tissue "crisscross" to form scar tissue, which, in turn, pulls on fibers farther down the line, and so on. This is because fascia interpenetrates all the body's internal structures in one contiguous, super-strong web. When I looked in the mirror, I could see the external effects of this internal distortion. My left shoulder was higher than my right. The left side of my ribcage protruded. My left breast was hoisted up several inches, climbing higher and becoming tighter over time. It was like wearing a permanent push-up bra—but only on one side! Not only could I see these fascial constrictions, I could feel them. When I stretched my left arm up, there was a tugging sensation all the way down into the front of my left thigh.

## The physical body displays its fascial condition.

Every human has some level of fascial distortion. It occurs in the course of living a life where we inevitably get injured, have surgeries, or experience physical or emotional pain. If you lie down on the floor and take a few minutes to relax, you may be able to start feeling the fascial restrictions in your own body. You may notice that one foot rolls out farther than the other. Or one arm turns in slightly. Maybe your head rolls a little to one side. The pelvis may be uneven. The physical body displays its fascial condition. If you tune into the subtle sensations in your body, you can begin to feel these particular restrictions, just as I did when I raised my arm up but felt a pulling down in my thigh.

Long before I had cancer, a trusted yoga client of mine introduced me to Dave, a lighthearted, masterful body therapist with decades of experience in physical education, physical therapy, and complementary body systems. He uses several different techniques, but for me the most important has been *myofascial release*, which works specifically with the fascia that weaves through every muscle. *Myo* refers to muscle and *fascia* to connective tissue. In this technique, the therapist gently compresses an area of restriction in the body, holding for up to several minutes until a release is felt beneath the superficial layers of skin. The therapist then follows that release to the next point of restriction, and so on. This sustained compression activates a biochemical change in the cells of the myofascia, loosening and releasing the knots of scar tissue. Think of it like slowly warming up Silly Putty until it becomes soft and mobile.

When I first met Dave, he explained that once a fascial restriction is released, it stays that way permanently. Which means the dysfunction or discomfort caused by that restriction is gone for good. I didn't understand this.

"How can it possibly be permanent? Won't it just spring back to the old position after a while?"

He gave me a perfect illustration.

"Have you ever seen those gauges that people put in their ears to make progressively larger holes? The gauges distort the fascia of the earlobes, and once that happens, if you remove the gauge, the earlobe just droops. It doesn't spring back to normal. And it never will. That's how fascia works."

In the case of a droopy earlobe, it's not a great feature. But in the case of restrictions that pull the body out of alignment and cause pain, it's a great thing that the released fascia stays released.

Now *that* made sense to me. I could picture it. But I had another question.

"If you get injured again, or have some kind of trauma to the body, fascial restrictions will return, right?"

Dave said, "The old restrictions will never return. But, sure, a new injury results in new restrictions. That's why every being on the planet can benefit from myofascial release! The idea is that, over time, we can release a great deal of these restricted areas and people will maintain their health naturally. Misalignments that cause pain, which, in turn, can lead to weakened muscles or cause people to lose their balance can be resolved." Dave is passionate about his calling, to say the least!

It took about two months of weekly appointments before I started to feel any changes. This is because myofascial release takes time. In a one-hour appointment, Dave might spend up to thirty minutes on just one area of the body. Early on I couldn't really "feel" what was happening during the treatments. So Dave demonstrated in a way that made it clear. You can feel it for yourself right now:

Place your hand (the full palm and fingers) on the skin of your sternum (it won't work over clothing, so make sure you're touching skin) and compress lightly, just enough to feel a "spring" beneath the skin.

Maintaining the compression, move the skin upward, in the direction of your head.

Now move it downward, in the direction of your navel.

Go back and forth, slowly. Chances are one direction will feel relatively "free" and the other may feel tight or stuck. You've just felt the fascia covering your sternum.

Keep your palm in place where you felt the most restriction. Don't force it, just "hang out there," as Dave says. Try keeping gentle compression without over-tensing your hand. Breathe calmly as you do this.

After about two minutes, you may begin to feel the edge of that restriction softening. Allow your palm to move along with that release until you feel the next boundary. Don't force the movement, just go with it.

Of course, there's much more to myofascial release than can be explained here, but this is the basic premise. During my sessions, I began to really feel the process as it was happening. For example, one day, Dave started at a spot where the restriction was quite noticeable, on my ribcage under my left arm. When he compressed there and moved into the fascial boundary, I could feel a tugging up through my shoulder and neck. He held the tissue for several minutes, then, gradually, I felt a release. It was like someone had loosened a belt. He continued until there was even more release over the whole area.

I began to get very interested in fascia. So interested that I decided to train in myofascial release myself. I thought it would make a great complement to yoga therapy. If I could offer someone a personal yoga practice to do for themselves at home, and supplement it with hands-on treatments in areas of restriction in the body, that might be a winning combination.

I had attended my first myofascial release training in June 2019. Two months later, I was diagnosed with cancer, and my hands-on training was put on hold. Eventually, 18 months later, after chemo, radiation, and the COVID vaccine, I was finally able to return to Dave for weekly myofascial release treatments and my experiential training resumed, this time with a whole new set of fascial restrictions for him to work on.

Dave ends every session by informing me that my job is to "go play and have fun!" It may sound goofy, but he truly means it. He has dedicated his career to the belief that all people deserve to be comfortable in their bodies, to move easily and enjoy life. After a few months, I began to notice more freedom in my movements. It was gradual but progressive, and it kept improving. It was a fantastic feeling! I continue to see him to this day.

After every appointment with Dave, I smile as I read the name of his therapy practice on a wooden sign outside his office: "Myofascial Freedom." A perfect name for what he gives people.

## HOW YOGA HELPED

At my first appointment with Dave before my cancer treatment, I didn't feel the fascia in my body. I just felt "good" when the session was over. But, soon, I began to tap into what yoga had taught me about sensing different levels of the body—muscles and bones, breath, and the subtle energetic vibration of the nervous system. It's like lying down outside on a starry night. At first, you only see the brightest stars. But, if you wait long enough, gradually you'll see more and more, thousands of stars becoming visible. In this way, as my sessions went on, I had a new sense of what was underneath the skin. If Dave worked on my hip, I'd feel something in my toes. If he worked on my shoulder, I might feel "the fascial voice" in my thigh.

It wasn't just on the treatment table where this awareness emerged. It came out during my yoga practice too, in what I called "fascial freedom" moments where my body led the way. The first time I experienced this was a few days after my lumpectomy. While resting on my back at the end of the practice, my left

arm began gently rolling back and forth. Then it sped up and began gyrating. All of this movement was spontaneous. I was completely conscious of what was happening, but I wasn't "in the driver's seat." There was a moment or two when I found myself thinking, *Am I just making this happen?* But I retreated from thinking and sank back into observation.

According to physical therapist John F. Barnes,[1] who developed the approach to myofascial release that Dave uses and that I began to study, this kind of movement is called "unwinding." Barnes' theory is that unwinding is the spontaneous, intuitive result of injured or restricted fascia "undoing" whatever happened at the time of injury. It could have been either a physical or emotional injury.

During that yoga practice, my arm continued to roll and spiral, speeding up then slowing down. Finally, my whole body settled into stillness. As I lay there, taking in the sensations I was feeling, it occurred to me that my left arm had been belted in place in a very similar position during the surgery a few days earlier. Maybe the fascia in my arm was releasing or "unwinding" after that restraint? The Barnes myofascial approach posits that however unwinding occurs in a person's body is the exact right way for that person. Who knows? Maybe this was how my body was "shaking off" the experience of the surgery. I pulled my trusty companion *vairagya*—nonattachment—out of my yoga toolbox and resisted the temptation to land on any concrete decision about what had just happened. I took it as an experience: My arm moved and gyrated in a way that felt completely spontaneous, then it settled down and I felt gentle energy pulsing through my body. That's what happened.

I experienced this "unwinding" again a few weeks later. I was resting in relaxation at the end of my morning yoga practice. I could feel tightness here and there. My left hand pulled inward more than the right; my right foot and leg were sort of stuck in position, whereas on the left they relaxed outward more naturally. I could sense, beneath the skin, the connective tissue restrictions that made my body end up in this particular position.

Slowly, my head began to roll back and forth. I could feel the subtle tug of fascia, on one side of my neck, almost like a "sting" as opposed to the bulkier feeling of muscle stretching. Then my head stayed turned to that side and began to move back and forth like I was shaking my head "no" with tiny movements. The effect traveled down my arm and into my fingers.

What I was feeling was the fascial body-stocking, pulling here, giving there. It felt very natural to remain completely relaxed and observe what my body needed to do. This head rolling went on for several minutes. Sometimes it sped up or slowed down in an irregular rhythm. Sometimes my head would lift up off the floor and my chin would reach down toward my chest. I'm sure it would have looked ridiculous if someone had walked in at that particular moment! Afterwards, as I lay still, I remembered a time when I was 16 and had fainted. I fell straight back and hit my head, sustaining a whiplash injury. Maybe my body was releasing some fascial restrictions from that old injury.

I allowed this spontaneous movement to happen whenever it presented itself during my yoga practices. The unwinding was playing as much a part in helping my body as my carefully planned yoga postures. In fact, the two practices could not be separated now that I had "connected with my connective tissue." But I remained deliberate about *vairāgya*—nonattachment—letting go of any need to claim what was happening during unwinding, and instead taking it as a spontaneous, intuitive experience. My body was "doing what came naturally," and I had faith that this was somehow healing for me personally.

## HOW OTHERS CAN HELP

The principles of myofascial release make sense to me, both intellectually and experientially. I'm not out to convert anyone, but I would certainly recommend giving it a try if you are having residual tightness anywhere in your body as a result of your cancer treatments, or from any injury whatsoever. There is a website listed in Resources at the end of the book for finding qualified therapists throughout the country. I'm sure you've figured out by now that it is a long process, so if you embark on it, have patience. The body usually doesn't operate like a light switch—on/off in an instant. It's more like baking a cake. It takes the amount of time it takes. If you pull it out too soon, you get a runny mess. If you allow for the required time, you get something really good.

# CHAPTER 20

# THE GIFT THAT KEEPS ON GIVING

*"Whether the notes of life are short or long;*
*from end to end what matters is the song."*

MARGERY WRIGHT MILLER

By 2023, my cancer treatments were three years behind me. During that time, my daughter graduated from college, moved to New York, and began her career as an interior designer. My son and his wonderful bride were married on a gorgeous June day and they settled in Brooklyn. I moved from New Jersey to Connecticut to be closer to Andy and to start our non-commuting life. And I returned to teaching yoga. It felt great to be back at work, doing what I truly love.

Along with all those good things, I had daily reminders of cancer. First, by way of a chemo drug many women take after breast cancer which suppresses estrogen. That amazing chemical reaction is keeping more cancer from growing inside me, so it's nonnegotiable as far as I'm concerned. But, stripping away estrogen every day has its inconveniences. Dry skin, dry hair, dry nails, dry bones (which requires another strong medication to deter osteoporosis), dry everything! Thinning hair, eyebrows, eyelashes.

Interrupted sleep. Flattened mood. Hot flashes a go-go.

I continued myofascial release treatments to help loosen the tightness in my neck, arm, and ribcage, which spiraled to my pelvis and legs, and to work on the main attraction: one very wonky left breast. I felt real progress, yet that breast seemed to inch higher and higher on my chest, even as the right one was sinking lower and lower! It was a challenge to find a bra that could balance things out. I began wearing more loose, flowing tops to camouflage the "up and down" look. Eventually, I got a prosthetic insert which fills up the flattened lower part of my left breast, so now I look balanced again (at least when I'm wearing a bra and clothing!).

I was experiencing "the gift that keeps on giving," a tongue-in-cheek description of radiation. It was clear what I'd seen as a recovery marathon was actually the "new normal." Remember when that phrase had its moment during the pandemic? We all had to learn to live with something we hadn't anticipated.

Life throws us curve balls all the time. Or, more precisely, we are very good at failing to see that curve balls are forever part of the game.

But from a yogic perspective, "new normal" is not a new idea. It relates to a concept called *pratipakṣa bhāvanam*, which is a method for shifting your state of mind by consciously substituting the opposite state. (*Pratipakṣa* means *the opposite* and *bhāvanam* means *condition* or *state of mind*.) For example, fear might be overcome by focusing sincerely on its opposite, courage. Or hate may be diffused by dwelling in feelings of love. Life throws us curve balls all the time. Or, more precisely, we are very good at failing to see that curve balls are forever part of the game. Things will always change. Like when I didn't know I had cancer one day and the next day I did know. One measure of our mettle could be said to reside in how we handle these challenges. *Pratipakṣa bhāvanam* gives us a template for relating to change, offers a choice about how to respond. My yoga teacher, Gary, relates it to the modern psychological idea of "cognitive reframing," looking at our circumstances from a different perspective. When I practice *pratipakṣa bhāvanam*, I like to envision myself literally standing up, turning around, and looking at my situation from the opposite side of the room.

So, here I was, three years after my cancer was "over," but still dealing with it. I had to ask myself, *How do I want to think about cancer? How do I want to feel about it? What effect do I want this entire experience to have on my life?*

The truth is, I'm still pondering these questions. I learned so much about myself as a result of this huge curve ball. It knocked me down a few pegs, showed me that a lot of the stuff I used to worry about was not worth it. My wonderful stepdad, Edward, likes to quote adages, and one of his classics is, *"Don't sweat the small stuff. P.S. It's all small stuff."*

I certainly have more patience than I used to about small details. I hardly ever correct other people's grammar in their emails or texts anymore (note I did say *hardly*!). That may sound facetious, but it's actually a true change for me. I can feel myself choosing not to respond in ways I used to, which always had to do with my personal way of controlling the little part of the world surrounding me. Now, I find more satisfaction in letting it go. The next step toward self-actualization, of course, is to evolve past that self-satisfaction and let others' grammar choices simply be there without any emotional attachment on my part. That would be pure equanimity!

That's a humorous example, but I'm hopeful about making bigger changes. I've been able to let go of relationship snags that I used to hang onto and replay in my mind. Maybe you've been there. A friend or family member or coworker says or does something that rubs you the wrong way, and you mentally rewrite the scene so you have the perfect reply, which manages to make you sound gracious, but also lets you *be right!*

Thankfully, the alchemy of cancer, yoga, and aging have helped me realize this: I just don't always know what other people are thinking or feeling. I'm enjoying the freedom that comes from saying to myself, *I don't know, so let me step back and observe for a minute.* It's allowed me to become more open, forgiving, and compassionate, not only of others, but mostly of myself, because I keep making mistakes. Even as I'm growing as a human. Like we all are.

Going through cancer also helped loosen up my comfort in connecting right away with people about life's deeper issues. When I was younger, I would think, *How do I know what to start talking about with this person? I don't want to invade their privacy or just assume I can ask about their life.* Now, I have more years and more confidence to know, *Everyone has gone through something. It will be okay if I say something sincere.*

Nowhere has this been more important than with my kids and loved ones. This experience forced me to say the important things in my heart, even when it felt uncomfortable. For some of us, telling our loved ones how much they mean to us not only summons joy, but also fear and major vulnerability. Because admitting how much we cherish them somehow also points out that life on earth is temporary. That's a hard reality. Even though we all know that life spans from birth to death, we still do an amazing job of denying the death part. I don't want to do that anymore. It's made me start making some plans and writing them down for my kids. They know I want my ashes to be scattered a year after I die (so everyone is over their extreme grief!), at a certain spot, with a certain song playing, and everyone telling a funny story about me. I want them to feel comfortable about my dying. So it's part of my life, not just a sad coda that everyone tries to deny and muscle through at the end. I've had some wonderful examples of beautiful end-of-life situations, and like those loved ones, I want to make mine an open affair. It's sad, it's happy, it's all things.

## HOW YOGA HELPED

*Pratipakṣa bhāvanam* is an indispensable strategy in the yoga toolkit. When I feel resistance about something, when I find myself wanting other people to do things differently, or circumstances to be different than they are, when I feel that frustration building up, this yoga technique helps me stop and say to myself, *Wait a minute. What's going on here? Who has the problem—everyone else? Or me?*

### How I Use This Yoga Tool

1. First, I do a short breath and movement practice, a few exercises to focus my attention and release physical tension. This gets my mind off the inner dialog that perpetuates the resistance and frustration.

2. Then comes a short breathing practice, or *prāṇāyāma*, to balance my nervous system (turn off any residual stress response), shift my attention further inward, and quiet my mind.

3. From there, I can meditate on the root of my frustration. This meditation is not trancelike or otherworldly. Rather, it lets me focus without distraction or subjective mental chatter.

4. From that dispassionate state, I make a conscious choice about how to handle my frustration. It lets me mentally outline what I'll do to transform that resistance into its opposite.

# CHAPTER 21

# HOW YOGA KEEPS HELPING

My yoga practice changed during my cancer treatments. I felt a new type of connection to myself and life that had nothing to do with the postures I was supposed to do, or the breath work, or the chants. It was simply a coming to terms with, *This is what they've been telling us all along. Life is short.*

My practice had become *sādhana* (pronounced *SAH* duh na), a Sanskrit word that means, among other definitions, a "discipline performed for the attainment of inner experience and self-realization."[1] It was a sanctuary for me at that time. Not a place to go and forget my troubles, but rather a time to be as fully present and human as I'd probably ever felt

before. A lot of the time during my *sādhana*, especially during chemo, I felt really sad. Or tired. Not just from the chemo, but tired from working at staying present and staying positive.

Looking back on it, I was in the midst of really changing some things about myself. Or, more accurately, getting through the muck that had covered up what was always there. Yoga teaches that we all have a light inside us that gets covered up by schmutz, a buildup of residue left by the experiences we go through but may not have fully processed. Yoga becomes a practice of cleaning away the schmutz, little by little. At the time of my cancer, I was doing a lot of cleaning.

"Our daily practice does not return us to the exact place we started. The practice has changed us."

**T.K.V. DESIKACHAR**

Another thing that made my *sādhana* unique at that time was the fact that I had turned myself over

completely to self-care. I had the enormous privilege of being able to take time off work for seven months to do nothing but go to chemo, then radiation, and to settle in at home, taking care of myself. I recognize how rare and lucky that is. I only wish every person could have the time they need to be treated and recover without having to work, support themselves or a family, just for those few months. That's what our healthcare system should be providing.

My yoga practice was as long as it needed to be on any given day. I had no other tasks pulling me away, urging me to finish up so that I could get to my desk or to the laundry or the grocery store. Between Andy, my sister Grace, and my friends, I was taken care of with food and any other necessities. Some people might think just staying home and having cancer would suck, and I'll admit, I'd rather not have had to do it at all. But since I had the cancer anyway, staying home and tending to my health was really a blessing.

Fast forward a couple years after the cancer. I realized one morning, *Boy, I've really let my yoga practice slip.* It had gotten shorter, more perfunctory. I still asked myself every day, *What do I need today?* But the answer had become more about releasing neck tension and less about connecting with deep inner stillness.

Here I was, back to being a regular human, blind to the inevitability of life's true course! Okay, so we probably all need a certain degree of suspended reality when it comes to day-to-day living. But there are so many reminders out there that life is short, and there's no getting yesterday back. It makes sense to find a way to keep that awareness at the forefront of our minds, our actions, our words, and feelings—and to do so without becoming bleak or morose.

That was what I needed to access every day, even if my post-cancer busy mind thought it needed to get to my desk or to the laundry. Nope. I needed to reignite that intention to slow down, breathe, and recognize the true and actual preciousness of this moment. To do the work for real, not just give it lip service. Or in the case of yoga, "thought service." See, a lot of us yogis are guilty of *thinking* about yoga a lot. But there's nothing worthwhile except to *do* the practice.

As I write the final words here, I don't feel the same rawness or sense of immediacy as when I wrote the first chapter. At that time, I felt a need to put my experiences down on paper as quickly as possible, to get it out there, no time to waste. Now, more than four years later, I don't have imminent mortality at the front of my mind. But that reality *is* there at the back of my mind, and I may be a few steps closer to making friends with it.

I'm glad I took a few years to complete this book, because it provided enough time to reflect on the real ebbs and flows of the broader experience, not just the acute, treatment time. If you're reading this as you go through cancer treatment, I hope you'll be able to see a broader picture too. To see the paradoxes in this life and still find its pure, unqualified joy. There is truth when we smile and laugh, even though circumstances are hard, even dire. Of all the tenets of yoga philosophy, I leave you with this one: *We have the capacity to know true joy, and to know that it comes from within.*

CHAPTER 22

# YOGA PRACTICES

*You don't have to have it all figured out to move forward. Just take one step.*
ANONYMOUS

The yoga practices in this chapter are simplified versions of those I used during cancer treatment, based on my study and practice of Viniyoga. They are "integrated practices," which means they weave together several elements of yoga, like movement, breath work, focus and concentration, meditation, and ritual.

Viniyoga combines breath and movement. If you're new to coordinating your breath with each movement, give it time and patience. When I first tried it, I thought it was for the birds, as my Nana Weinsheimer would say! However, after about two weeks, I realized something:

I felt damn good at the end of these practices! The reason is because coordinating breath and movement is the starting point to experiencing a calm, focused body and mind. Only when I transform into that state can I unplug from my surface-level, default mindset and settle into my "heart-mind," where I can more clearly address life's challenges, mysteries, and joys.

Feel free to use only the elements in these practices that feel natural to you. Shorter versions of the practices are offered at the end of each one. Make the practices yours!

## GUIDELINES FOR YOGA PRACTICE

- Check with your doctor(s) before beginning any exercise routine, especially post-surgery.

- Always proceed with awareness and caution. Practice according to that day's condition. Never push beyond your limits.

- Modify as needed. This may include, but isn't limited to, adjusting: body position, breath instructions, exertion level, number of repetitions, number of postures overall, chanting softly or not at all.

- Practice on an empty stomach (at least two hours after eating). First thing in the morning is ideal.

- You can practice on the floor or on your bed. Wear any clothes that allow comfortable movement.

- There are options for shorter versions at the end of each practice.

## NOTES ON BREATH FOR ALL PRACTICES

- Breathe smoothly and comfortably at all times. Never force your breath. No matter what the instructions say, adjust your breathing to your condition on that day.

- If possible, use the *ujjayi* valve, that soft hiss at the throat, as you breathe throughout the practice. This helps slow down and lengthen the breath, which adds to the relaxation effect. (It feels like you are lightly "dragging" the breath through the throat, and may sound like a light snore or a quiet Darth Vader!)

- If it's comfortable, gently draw the navel in on the exhalations.

- Remember that breath is a key link between the body's functions and our state of mind and emotion. Even if you find it difficult to sync up the breath with the movements, just using soft, smooth breathing will bring benefits.

- In the meditations, you'll see instructions to "Imagine a 'central channel' running through the center of your body, from the crown of your head to the root at the pelvic floor."

  » You can think of this as a roadway for your attention.

  » In any way that works for you, imagine or feel your breath flowing down through that central channel as you inhale and back up as you exhale.

    – This may sound confusing to some people, if they mistakenly think of the inhalation as an upward movement and the exhalation as a downward movement, like when the doctor says, "Take a deep breath," and you hoist up your chest and shoulders to inhale, then drop them to exhale.

    – But consider this: On inhalation, air flows **in and down** into the lungs. On exhalation, it flows **up and out**. So, try to follow each breath, from crown to root (top down) on the inhalation as the torso expands, and from root to crown (bottom up) on the exhalation as you pull in the navel. If you get off-track, simply start over. That's part of the practice, and everyone does it!

# SAMPLE GO-TO PRACTICE

*Suggested time to do this practice: morning or afternoon*

My go-to practice was a staple of self-care as I went through cancer treatment. I practiced it in some form almost every day, even if I did just one yoga posture and a few rounds of breath practice. Below is a sample you can use to build your own personal practice. Adjust the elements to fit your needs and condition. And if you want help creating a personal practice, you can reach out to me at:

info@windingpathyoga.com

## SET A THEME

Think about the quality you want to embody. Keep it simple. Examples might be: *love, strength, faith, light, peace, balance.*

*Write your personal theme here:*

_____

## OPENING

RITUAL IS LIKE A WAKE-UP CALL TO THE PRESENT MOMENT.

1. An opening ritual shifts the mindset; it's like a "wake-up" call to the present moment. If you have items like these on an altar, ring the chime and light the candle and/or incense. Pause to let your senses take in the sound, light, and/or smell.

2. Sitting or lying down, take three simple breaths in and out through your nose. Acknowledge inwardly, *I am beginning my practice now.*

BEGIN YOUR PRACTICE WITH INTENTION

## INNER FOCUS

Here, you shift attention from external to internal.

1. Sit comfortably or lie down.

2. Do the steps below with an open mind, not analyzing or judging. This takes practice, so don't worry if your mind feels busy at first.

   - **Body:** Scan from top to bottom and notice what you feel: contact with the floor, chair, or bed; alignment of body parts; sensations (tension, ease, tingling, warmth, coolness, etc.). It may help to name, mentally, the things you feel, like *shoulder tension* or *left foot rolls out.*

   - **Thoughts/Emotions:** Notice the thoughts or emotions that come and go in your mind. Stand back like an observer without engaging in the inner conversation. You can say, mentally, *That's impatience* or *That's planning.*

   - **Breath:** Notice each breath as it comes in and out through your nose. Make a soft hiss at the throat to slow down and smooth out the breath (it feels as if are gently "dragging" the breath through the throat, which you are!). On each inhalation, let the torso expand. On each exhalation, gently draw the navel in. Continue for 5 rounds of breath.

   - **Chant:** If you like chanting and find that sound vibration lifts your mood or energy, incorporate a chant into your practice. Don't worry about a specific tune; this is just for you. Examples for a go-to practice might be: *I know my strength; Let the sun shine; Faith, courage, and wisdom; Ave Maria; Love, love, love,* or *Oṁ,* which represents our ever-present consciousness.

   *Write your chant here:*

   _____

   _____

   _____

   - **Chant your word or phrase 3 times.** For example, if you were using the phrase *I know my strength,* you would:

     » Inhale smoothly.

     » On exhale, chant ***I know my strength*** (make it last about 6 seconds)

   - **Reflect** on your theme. You might ask yourself, *How can* Strength *help me today? What form of* Strength *do I need?* Take a few moments to sit with your question; no need to answer right now.

## MOVEMENT

Now you begin the yoga postures for this practice, shown on the following pages. Be sure to modify the exercises for your needs, or skip those which are not useful or safe for you on any given day.

# 1. KNEES TO CHEST POSE (GENTLY STRETCHES LOW BACK; MASSAGES COLON)

1. Begin in Position A. Let the feet and legs relax; the arms do the work in this pose. **Inhale** here.

POSITION A: INHALE HERE

2. **Exhale**, gently draw the navel in as you bring the knees closer to the torso, as in Position B. Feel your low back press into the floor.

POSITION B: EXHALE TO THIS POSITION

3. **Repeat 6–8 times.** Make your breath and movements flow together smoothly.

# 2. SUPINE LEG STRETCH (STRETCHES BACK OF LEGS; IMPROVES CIRCULATION)

**1.** Begin in Position A.

POSITION A: START HERE

**2. Inhale** and extend legs upward, as in Position B. You can also do this exercise one leg at a time. It's fine if your knees don't straighten all the way. Just stretch comfortably without causing your back to arch up.

POSITION B: INHALE TO THIS POSITION

**3. Exhale** to Position A.

**4. Repeat 3–6 times.** Make your breath and movements flow together smoothly.

# 3A. BRIDGE POSE (STRENGTHENS LEGS, HIPS, CORE; ARTICULATES THE SPINE; STRETCHES THE CHEST AND UPPER BACK; BUILDS FOCUS)

**1.** Begin in Position A.

POSITION A: START HERE

**2. Inhale**, press your feet into the floor and raise the pelvis to Position B. Rest on your upper back and shoulders, *not on your neck*. Squeeze the buttocks for stability.

INHALE TO THIS POSITION

**3. Exhale**, gently draw the navel in and lower the spine vertebrae-by-vertebrae to Position A. Try to keep a backward pelvic tilt all the way through the exhale movement so the lower spine rolls onto the mat as you come down.

**4. Repeat 3–6 times.** Make your breath and movements flow together smoothly.

# 3B. BRIDGE POSE – ALTERNATING ARMS

**1.** Begin in Position A.

POSITION A: START HERE

**2. Inhale**, press your feet into the floor to raise the pelvis, and take both arms overhead, as in Position B. Rest on your upper back and shoulders, *not on your neck*. Squeeze the buttocks.

POSITION B: INHALE TO HERE

**3. Exhale** and draw in the navel as you lower the spine and **left** arm, turning the head **left**, as in Position C. Try to make the spine, arm, and head all move in concert.

POSITION C: EXHALE TO HERE

**4. Inhale** to Position B.

POSITION B: INHALE TO HERE

5. **Exhale** and draw in the navel as you lower the spine and **right** arm, turning the head **right**, as in Position D.

**POSITION D: EXHALE TO HERE**

6. **Repeat the sequence for 3–4 rounds.** End at Position A.

# 4. SWEEPING ARMS/CHILD POSE, WITH OPTIONAL CHANTING

(BRINGS CIRCULATION TO UPPER BACK, NECK, SHOULDERS; STRETCHES LOW BACK; STRENGTHENS CORE; CHANTING ENHANCES FOCUS AND CONNECTION TO THEME)

*Caution: Get your doctor's clearance if you have osteoporosis of the spine.*

**1.** Begin in Position A.

POSITION A: START HERE

**2.** On **inhale**, initiate movement between the shoulder blades to begin simultaneously lifting arms, upper back, chest, and head, as in Position B.

POSITION B: INHALE TO BEGIN UPWARD SWEEPING MOTION

**3.** Continue **inhaling** through the upward motion of the arms and body, as in Positions C, D, and E. This should be one smooth motion, with the arms sweeping wide.

POSITIONS C, D, AND E: CONTINUE SWEEPING THE ARMS UP

4. Complete the **inhalation** at the top of the movement, with the arms overhead, as in Position F. If it's difficult to do one continuous inhalation, just breathe smoothly and naturally.

**POSITION F: COMPLETE THE INHALATION HERE**

5. **Exhale** and sweep the arms wide to begin the reverse movement, as in Positions E, D, C, and B. This should be one smooth motion. If it's uncomfortable to do one continuous exhalation, just breathe smoothly and naturally.

   *Option:* **Chant on exhalation.**

6. Complete the **exhalation** at Position A.

7. **Repeat the sequence 3–6 times.**

## 5. COBRA POSE (STRENGTHENS UPPER BACK, CORE; LIFTS ENERGY LEVEL)

**1.** Begin in Position A.

POSITION A: START HERE

**2. Inhale** and traction your palms downward to elongate your chest forward and up, as in Position B. You don't have to lift very high. Use your back muscles to lift your chest, rather than doing a push-up with the arms or pulling up with the head and neck. Gently tighten the legs and buttocks to stabilize your low back.

POSITION B: INHALE TO THIS POSITION

**3. Exhale** to Position A.

**4. Repeat 3–6 times.**

# 6. LOCUST POSE (STRENGTHENS UPPER BACK, CORE, BUTTOCKS, LEGS; LIFTS ENERGY LEVEL)

1. Begin in Position A.

POSITION A: START HERE

2. **Inhale** and traction your palms downward to elongate your chest forward and up, and raise the **right** leg, as in Position B. Elongate the lifted leg and squeeze at the crease of the buttock to isolate the working muscles.

POSITION B: INHALE TO THIS POSITION (RIGHT LEG LIFTED)

3. **Exhale** to Position A.

POSITION A: EXHALE TO THIS POSITION

4. **Inhale**, repeat with the **left** leg, as in Position C.

POSITION C: INHALE TO THIS POSITION (LEFT LEG LIFTED)

5. **Exhale** to Position A.

6. Repeat the sequence 3 times.

# 7. TABLETOP/CHILD POSE, WITH OPTIONAL CHANTING

(ARTICULATES THE SPINE, STRETCHES LOWER BACK; COMPENSATES FOR PREVIOUS BACK BENDING POSTURES; CHANTING ENHANCES CONNECTION TO THEME)

**1.** Begin in Position A.

POSITION A: START HERE

**2. Inhale** and begin to simultaneously lift chest and head, as in Position B.

POSITION B: INHALE TO BEGIN COMING FORWARD

**3.** Continue the **inhalation** as you come to all fours, chest lifted, as in Position C. Draw the shoulders away from the ears. Avoid overarching the spine. If it's uncomfortable to do one continuous inhalation, just breathe smoothly and naturally.

POSITION C: COMPLETE THE INHALATION HERE

**4. Exhale** and begin to reverse the movement, as in Position D.

*Option:* **Chant on exhalation.**

POSITION D: EXHALE TO BEGIN MOVING BACK

5. As you complete the **exhalation**, return to Position A by bowing to the forearms, then lowering the head, and finally settling hips to heels.

POSITION A: COMPLETE THE EXHALATION HERE

6. Repeat 3–6 times.

## 8A. MOUNTAIN POSE (STRETCHES FULL BODY; STRENGTHENS LEGS, CORE; BUILDS BALANCE AND FOCUS; LIFTS ENERGY LEVEL; CHANTING ENHANCES CONNECTION TO THEME)

**1.** Begin in Position A.

POSITION A: START HERE

**2. Inhale** and raise your heels as you sweep your **right** arm up and your **left** arm halfway, as in Position B. It's fine to keep the feet on the floor, as well!

POSITION B: INHALE TO THIS POSITION (RIGHT ARM UP/LEFT ARM HALFWAY)

**3. Exhale** to Position A. Try to coordinate the movement so the arms and heels lands at the same time (but don't worry if that doesn't happen at first!).

**4. Inhale** and raise your heels as you sweep your **left** arm up and your **right** arm halfway, as in Position C.

POSITION A: EXHALE TO THIS POSITION

POSITION C: INHALE TO THIS POSITION (LEFT ARM UP/RIGHT ARM HALFWAY)

**5. Exhale** to Position A.

**6.** Repeat the sequence 3 times.

# 8B. MOUNTAIN POSE, WITH HOLD AFTER INHALE AND OPTIONAL CHANTING

**1.** Begin in Position A.

POSITION A: START HERE

**2.** **Inhale**, raise your heels and sweep both arms overhead, as in Position B. It's fine to keep the feet on the floor, as well. **Hold for 2 seconds** in this position and feel the energy you are using!

POSITION B: INHALE TO THIS POSITION; HOLD 2 SECONDS

**3.** **Exhale** and lower the arms and heels to Position A. Try to coordinate the movement so the arms and heels land at the same time (but don't worry if that doesn't happen at first!)

*Option:* **Chant on exhalation.**

**4.** Repeat 3–6 times.

# 9. WARRIOR I, WITH OPTIONAL CHANTING (STRENGTHENS LEGS, BACK, SHOULDERS; LIFTS ENERGY LEVEL; CHANTING ENHANCES CONNECTION TO THEME)

**1.** Begin in Position A.

POSITION A: START HERE

**2.** **Inhale,** lunge, bending the **left** knee and stretch your arms wide, palms up, as in Position B. Stay grounded through the back foot; lean torso forward of the hips and stretch the chest. Avoid jutting the head forward.

POSITION B: INHALE TO THIS POSITION

**3.** **Exhale** to Position A.

*Option:* **Chant on exhalation.**

**4.** **Repeat for 3 rounds.**

**5.** Then **stay** in Position B as you **inhale** and stretch the arms wide.

POSITION B: INHALE IN THIS POSITION

**6.** **Exhale** and place your hands at the heart, as in Position C.

*Option:* **Chant on exhalation.**

POSITION C: EXHALE IN THIS POSITION

**7.** **Repeat Positions B–C for 3 rounds of breath.** On the final **exhalation,** return to Position A. Repeat entire sequence with the **right** leg forward.

# 10. STANDING FORWARD BEND (COMPENSATES FOR PREVIOUS BACK BENDING POSE; STRETCHES BACK OF BODY)

*Cautions: If you have low blood pressure, vertigo, or glaucoma, go between Position A and C only, keeping your head above your heart. Get your doctor's clearance if you have osteoporosis of the spine.*

**1.** Begin in Position A. **Inhale** here.

POSITION A: START HERE WITH AN INHALATION

**2.** **Exhale**, bend your knees slightly and slide your hands down the legs to any comfortable position (Position B). Relax the back of your neck; relax your shoulders away from your ears. Feel your spine gently rounding.

POSITION B: EXHALE TO THIS POSITION.

*Option:* Remain in Position B to breathe smoothly for a few rounds of breath.

**3.** **Inhale** and keep the slight bend in your knees as you lift the chest and head through Position C, pressing up through the legs and feet to stand all the way up to Position A. *(Hint: Think of coming up like a cobra, articulating up through the spine by lifting the chest and upper back first. Avoid "rolling up like a rag doll.")*

POSITION C: INHALE TO BEGIN COMING UP.

COMPLETE INHALATION HERE

**4.** **Repeat 3–6 times.**

# 11. STANDING SIDE STRETCH (STRETCHES SIDE OF BODY, SHOULDERS; STRENGTHENS CORE; HAS A REFRESHING EFFECT ON ENERGY LEVEL)

**1.** Begin in Position A.

**2. Inhale** and stretch your **right** arm up, as in Position B.

POSITION A: START HERE

POSITION B: INHALE TO THIS POSITION

**3. Exhale**, gently draw the navel in and stretch the **right** arm over, sliding the **left** arm down side of leg, as in Position C. Stretch directly to the side, not leaning forward.

**POSITION C: EXHALE TO THIS POSITION**

**4. Repeat Positions B–C 3 times; then hold Position C for 2–3 rounds of breath.** Release to Position A and repeat the sequence on the other side of the body.

# 12. CHILD TO TABLETOP TO DOWN DOG, WITH OPTIONAL CHANTING (STRENGTHENS ENTIRE BODY; STRETCHES ARMS, SHOULDERS, LEGS, BACK; HAS A REFRESHING EFFECT ON ENERGY LEVEL; CHANTING ENHANCES CONNECTION TO THEME)

**1.** Begin in Position A.

**POSITION A: START HERE**

**2.** **Inhale** and lift your chest and head, coming to Tabletop position. Draw the shoulders away from the ears. Avoid overarching the spine. At the end of the inhalation, curl the toes under (Position B).

**POSITION B: INHALE TO THIS POSITION**

**3.** **Exhale** and push away from the floor, raising your hips up and letting your head release into Down Dog, as in Position C. Keep a little bend in the knees. Spread your fingers and press the hands into the floor. Stretch your tailbone way up; stretch through your armpits!

*Option:* **Chant on exhalation**

**POSITION C: EXHALE TO THIS POSITION**

**4.** **Inhale** and lift your head and chest as you lower your knees to Position D, uncurling the toes.

**POSITION D: INHALE TO THIS POSITION**

**5. Exhale** and reverse the movement back to Position A.

*Option:* **Chant on exhalation.**

POSITION A: EXHALE TO THIS POSITION

**6. Repeat the sequence up to 3 times.** Take extra breaths, as needed, throughout the sequence.

## 13. SUPINE BUTTERFLY (STRETCHES AND STRENGTHENS INNER THIGHS, GROIN; EXERCISES SACROILIAC JOINT; HAS A CALMING EFFECT ON THE ENERGY LEVEL)

1. Begin in Position A.

POSITION A: START HERE

2. **Inhale** and take your knees outward, as in Position B.

POSITION B: INHALE TO THIS POSITION

3. **Exhale** and *slowly* bring the knees back together, as in Position A.

4. **Repeat 6 times.**

# 14. SUPINE TWIST (ROTATES SPINE; STRETCHES CHEST AND ARMS; HAS A REFRESHING EFFECT ON THE ENERGY LEVEL)

*Caution: You may want to skip this pose if you have sacrum pain.*

**1.** Begin in Position A. **Inhale** here.

POSITION A: START HERE WITH AN INHALATION

**2. Exhale**, twist your knees to the **right** and turn your head to the **left,** as in Position B. Adjust your arms, as needed, for shoulder comfort.

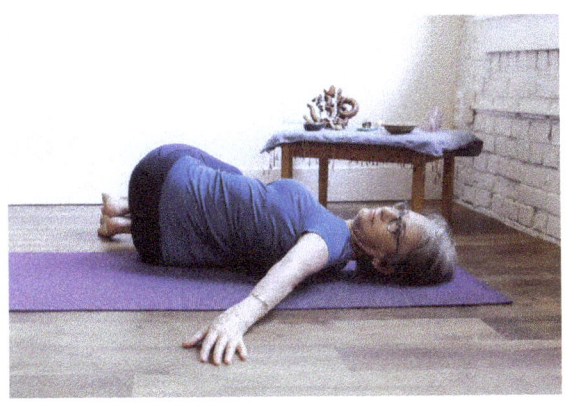

POSITION B: EXHALE TO THIS POSITION

**3. Inhale** to Position A.

POSITION A: INHALE TO THIS POSITION

**4. Exhale**, twist your knees to the **left,** and turn your head to the **right,** as in Position C. Adjust your arms as needed for shoulder comfort.

POSITION C: EXHALE TO THIS POSITION

**5. Inhale** to Position A.

**6.** Repeat the sequence 3 times.

# 15. KNEES TO CHEST POSE (REPEAT POSE 1 ABOVE)

## 16. RESTING POSE (ALLOWS THE BODY TO ABSORB THE EFFECTS OF THE PRACTICE; HAS A CALMING AND REFRESHING EFFECT ON THE ENERGY LEVEL)

1. Lie in Position A, B, or C. You can also lie on your bed.

POSITION A: RESTING POSE

POSITION B: RESTING POSE, BLANKET UNDER THE HEAD

POSITION C: RESTING POSE, BLANKET UNDER THE KNEES

2. Position your legs a little wider than hip width and your arms about 45 degrees from your body, palms up. Let your feet and legs relax and your fingers curl naturally. **Lie here for 5–10 minutes.** The body and mind benefit greatly from this time to absorb the benefits of the practice. Relaxation takes time, so give yourself that gift!

# BREATH PRACTICE (PRĀṆĀYĀMA)

1. Sit, as in Position A. You can also sit in a chair or lie on the floor or your bed.

**POSITION A: START HERE**

2. Take a moment to feel the sensation of your breath. Notice your body expanding as you inhale and relaxing as you exhale.

3. Imagine a "central channel" running through the center of your body, from the crown of your head to the root at the pelvic floor. This is like a roadway for your attention. Try to follow each breath, from crown to root (top down) on the inhalation as the torso expands, and from root to crown (bottom up) on the exhalation as you pull in the navel. If you get off-track, simply start over.

4. Once you've established that pattern of following the breath with your attention, **silently repeat your theme or chant with each inhalation and exhalation for nine rounds** (gradually work up to 12 rounds). You can keep track by touching your thumb to successive fingertips. If your mind wanders, just bring it back.

# MEDITATION

Everything up to this point has helped prepare you for meditation. By now, hopefully your body feels relaxed, your breath is smooth and quiet, and your mind is clear. Recall that meditation is holding your attention on a certain object and maintaining an open mind, free from judgement or the default "inner dialog" of our conditioning.

You may choose to simply sit in inner stillness, focusing on the soft, natural flow of your breath.

Or, you may want to use the "Cave of the Heart" visualization that I used. This is a yoga practice of meditation in our deepest heart. Take some time with each of the steps below.

1. Tune into the effects of your practice. Feel the circulation in your body from the movement and breath work. Feel a sense of peace after unplugging from the mind's ongoing chatter.

2. Picture yourself in the cave of your heart. Everyone pictures this special place differently, and whatever image appears is the right one. It might be a forest path, or a quiet beach, a mountain vista, or something else entirely.

3. Focus on the quality you want to cultivate with your personal theme. Sense that quality streaming like sunlight from the top of your head, down the central channel, into the cave of your heart where you are seated. For

example, if *Strength* is your theme, sense or feel *Strength* flowing down through the central channel, filling your heart and from there, flowing through your entire body. Actively focus on that quality for several minutes. Feel it in your own way.

4. Recognize that you already possess the quality; it's been there all along. Remember and reassure yourself that you have an innate capacity for inner well-being and joy despite any external conditions.

### CLOSING

When you sense yourself coming out of the meditative state, repeat your chant or verse three times, once silently, once softly, and once more loudly, to symbolize returning from the inner world to the outer. If you have altar items, extinguish the candle and ring the singing bowl. Listen until the vibrating chime has completely dissipated.

You may want to jot a few notes in a journal about your practice. I found it very helpful to put things into words. This brings purpose and intention to your practice and bolsters your commitment to caring for yourself.

### OPTIONS FOR SHORTER VERSIONS OF THE "GO-TO PRACTICE"

1. Opening; Inner Focus; Poses 1–4, 13, 15, 16; Breath Practice; Meditation

2. Opening; Inner Focus; Poses 1–7, 16; Breath Practice; Meditation

3. Opening; Inner Focus; Poses 1–3, 7–9, 12, 16; Breath Practice; Meditation

# PRACTICE FOR CONSTIPATION

*Suggested time to do this practice: first thing in the morning*

This practice focuses on yoga postures and breath, and works really well to keep things moving! The secret weapon is an emphasis on exhalation and holding the breath out after exhalation. These techniques massage the colon, bringing circulation to the area.

### Hints about Breath in This Practice

- Throughout the practice, use a soft hiss at the throat to create a "valve" which slows down the breath. Use this hiss on both the inhalation and exhalation.

- On exhalation, draw the navel in and hold it in.

- In some postures, the instructions will be to hold the breath out for several seconds after the exhalation. Again, keep the navel drawn in throughout that hold after exhale.

- In some cases, the instructions will be to move at the same time that you're holding the breath out after exhalation.

- During the seated breath practice at the end, you'll be using a two-part exhalation in which you will:

  » exhale half the breath, drawing in below the navel

  » hold

  » exhale the rest of the breath, drawing in above the navel

  » hold

  » inhale, expanding the chest first, then relaxing above the navel, and then below the navel in one smooth flow

  » repeat the sequence.

*Note: This is a strong practice.* It's best to skip it on days when you feel nauseous, overly fatigued, lightheaded, or short of breath. Be sure to stay in contact with your care team regarding constipation, especially during chemotherapy.

## MOVEMENT

The yoga postures for this practice are shown on the following pages. Be sure to modify the exercises for your needs, or skip those which are not useful or safe for you on any given day.

# 1. OPENING / RESTING POSE

**1.** Begin in Position A.

POSITION A

**2.** Center your attention: Notice/feel your body, your breath, and your state of mind. Mentally note, *I am starting my practice now.*

**3.** Place your hands on your belly. This area is associated with the "digestive fire," according to yoga tradition. Reflect on the food you've eaten recently. Acknowledge the value of good nutrition. Consider the marvelous complexity of the digestive system and its ability to separate what the body needs from what it doesn't need.

**4.** Begin to lengthen your breath. On each **exhalation**, draw the navel toward the spine.

*Continue for 10 rounds of breath.*

# 2. TABLETOP/CHILD POSE (MASSAGES THE COLON; ARTICULATES THE SPINE, STRETCHES LOWER BACK)

**1.** Begin in Position A.

POSITION A: START HERE

**2. Inhale** and begin to simultaneously lift chest and head, as in Position B.

POSITION B: INHALE TO BEGIN COMING FORWARD

**3.** Continue the **inhalation** as you come to all fours, chest lifted, as in Position C. Draw the shoulders away from the ears. Avoid overarching the spine. If it's uncomfortable to do one continuous inhalation, just breathe smoothly and naturally.

POSITION C: COMPLETE THE INHALATION HERE

**4. Exhale** and begin to reverse the movement, as in Position D.

POSITION D: EXHALE TO BEGIN MOVING BACK

**5.** As you complete the **exhalation**, return to Position A by bowing to the forearms, then lowering the head, and finally settling hips to heels.

POSITION A: COMPLETE THE EXHALATION HERE

**6.** Repeat 3–6 times.

## 3. COBRA POSE (STRENGTHENS UPPER BACK, CORE; LIFTS ENERGY LEVEL)

1. Begin in Position A.

POSITION A: START HERE

2. **Inhale** and traction your palms downward to elongate your chest forward and up, as in Position B. You don't have to lift very high. Use your back muscles to lift your chest, rather than doing a push-up with the arms or pulling up with the head and neck. Gently tighten the legs and buttocks to stabilize your low back.

POSITION B: INHALE TO THIS POSITION

3. **Exhale** to Position A.

4. **Repeat 3 times.**

5. Then **inhale** to Position B and **stay there for 3 rounds of breath.** On each **inhalation**, feel the belly press into the floor. On each **exhalation**, draw the navel toward the spine.

Release to Position A on **exhalation**.

# 4. TABLETOP/CHILD POSE, MOVING ON HOLD AFTER EXHALE
(MASSAGES THE COLON, ARTICULATES THE SPINE, STRETCHES LOWER BACK; COMPENSATES FOR PREVIOUS BACK BENDING POSE; HOLD AFTER EXHALE ENHANCES COLON MASSAGE)

1. Begin in Position A.

POSITION A: START HERE

2. **Inhale** and begin to simultaneously lift your chest and head, as in Position B.

POSITION B: INHALE TO BEGIN COMING FORWARD

3. Continue the **inhalation** as you come to all fours, chest lifted, as in Position C. Draw the shoulders away from the ears. Avoid overarching the spine. If it's uncomfortable to do one continuous inhalation, just breathe smoothly and naturally.

POSITION C: COMPLETE THE INHALATION HERE

4. **Exhale** and draw the navel in, **remaining** in Position C. When you've completed the **exhalation**, **hold** the breath out as you reverse the movement and return to Position A.

RETURN HERE AS YOU HOLD THE BREATH OUT AFTER EXHALE

5. Then take a few comfortable breaths in Child's Pose.

6. **Repeat the sequence 6 times.**

## 5. REVOLVED TRIANGLE POSE (ROTATES SPINE, RIBCAGE, SHOULDER GIRDLE; STRENGTHENS CORE; HAS A REFRESHING EFFECT ON THE ENERGY LEVEL)

*Caution: Skip this pose if it causes or exacerbates shoulder pain or sacrum pain. Get your doctor's clearance if you have osteoporosis of the spine.*

1. Place your hands on your belly and consider the amazing process of digestion.

2. Move to Position A. **Inhale** here.

POSITION A: INHALE IN THIS POSITION

PAUSE TO CONNECT WITH THE AREA OF DIGESTION

3. **Exhale** and take your **left** arm toward your **right** foot, and your **right** arm toward the sky (Position B). The head can be down, sideways, or up, based on your comfort level.

POSITION B: EXHALE TO THIS POSITION

4. **Inhale** to Position A.

POSITION A: INHALE TO THIS POSITION

5. **Exhale** and take your **right** arm toward the **left** foot, and the **left** arm toward the sky (Position C).

POSITION C: EXHALE TO THIS POSITION

6. **Inhale** to Position A.

7. **Repeat the sequence 3 times.**

8. **Then hold Position B for 3 breaths, followed by Position C for 3 breaths.**

    **Inhale** to Position A to end.

## 6. STANDING FORWARD BEND (COMPENSATES FOR PREVIOUS TWISTING POSE; STRETCHES BACK OF BODY)

*Caution: If you have low blood pressure, vertigo, glaucoma, go between Position A and C only, keeping your head above your heart. Get your doctor's clearance if you have osteoporosis of the spine.*

1. Begin in Position A. **Inhale** here.

POSITION A: START HERE WITH AN INHALATION

2. **Exhale**, bend your knees slightly and slide your hands down the legs to any comfortable position (Position B). Relax the back of your neck; relax your shoulders away from your ears. Feel your spine gently rounding.

POSITION B: EXHALE TO THIS POSITION.

*Option:* Remain in this position to breathe smoothly for a few rounds of breath.

**3.** **Inhale** and keep the slight bend in your knees as you lift the chest and head through Position C, pressing up through the legs and feet to stand all the way up to Position A. *(Hint: Think of coming up like a cobra, articulating up through the spine by lifting the chest and upper back first. Avoid "rolling up like a rag doll.")*

**4.** **Repeat 3–6 times.**

POSITION C: INHALE TO BEGIN COMING UP.

COMPLETE INHALATION HERE

# 7. TABLETOP TO CHILD POSE, MOVING ON HOLD AFTER EXHALE (REPEAT POSE 4 ABOVE)

# 8. SUPINE TWIST, MOVING ON HOLD AFTER EXHALE

(ROTATES SPINE; STRETCHES CHEST AND ARMS; HAS A REFRESHING EFFECT ON THE ENERGY LEVEL; HOLD AFTER EXHALE ENHANCES COLON MASSAGE)

**1.** Begin in Position A. **Inhale** here.

POSITION A: START HERE WITH AN INHALATION

**2. Exhale,** twist your knees to the **right** and turn your head to the **left,** as in Position B. Adjust your arms, as needed, for shoulder comfort.

POSITION B: EXHALE TO THIS POSITION

**3. Inhale** to Position A.

POSITION A: INHALE TO THIS POSITION

**4. Exhale,** twist your knees to the **left,** and turn your head to the **right,** as in Position C. Adjust your arms as needed for shoulder comfort.

POSITION C: EXHALE TO THIS POSITION

5. **Inhale** to Position A.

6. **Repeat the sequence 3 times.**

7. Next, **inhale** and **exhale** in Position A. When you've completed the **exhalation**, **hold** the breath out as you twist to the **right** (Position B).

8. **Inhale** to Position A and remain here to **exhale**. When you've completed the **exhalation**, **hold** the breath out as you twist to the **left** (Position C).

9. **Repeat this sequence 3 times,** alternating between Position B and C on the **hold after exhalation.**

10. **Inhale** to Position A to end.

# 9. SUPINE LEG STRETCH (COMPENSATES FOR PREVIOUS TWISTING POSE; STRETCHES BACK OF LEGS; IMPROVES CIRCULATION)

**1.** Begin in Position A.

POSITION A: START HERE

**2. Inhale** and extend legs upward, as in Position B. You can also do this exercise one leg at a time. It's fine if your knees don't straighten all the way. Just stretch comfortably without causing your back to arch up.

**3. Exhale** to Position A.

**4.** Repeat 3–6 times.

POSITION B: INHALE TO THIS POSITION

# 10. SEATED TWIST, HOLD AFTER EXHALE (MASSAGES THE COLON; ROTATES THE SPINE; STRENGTHENS THE CORE; HAS A REFRESHING EFFECT ON THE ENERGY LEVEL)

*Caution: Avoid this pose if you have osteoporosis of the spine.*

1. Begin in Position A, your right hand on your left knee, your left hand on floor behind the body. **Inhale** here.

POSITION A: START HERE WITH AN INHALATION

2. **Exhale** and twist to the **left,** as in Position B.

POSITION B: EXHALE TO THIS POSITION

3. **Inhale** to return to Position A.

4. **Repeat 3 times.** Then **stay** in Position B for 3 rounds of breath, **holding** the breath out for 2–3 seconds after each **exhalation.**

5. Then repeat the entire sequence to the opposite side (Positions C-D).

POSITION C: INHALE IN THIS POSITION

POSITION D: EXHALE TO THIS POSITION

6. **Inhale** to Position A to end.

# 11. KNEES TO CHEST POSE, HOLD AFTER EXHALE

(COMPENSATES FOR PREVIOUS TWIST; GENTLY STRETCHES LOW BACK; MASSAGES COLON)

1. Begin, as in Position A. **Inhale** here.

POSITION A: INHALE HERE

2. **Exhale**, gently draw the navel in as you bring the knees closer to the chest, as in Position B. Feel your low back press into the floor. **Hold** the breath out for 2–3 seconds after **exhalation.**

POSITION B: EXHALE TO THIS POSITION; HOLD FOR 2-3 SECONDS

3. Repeat 6–8 times.

# BREATH PRACTICE (PRĀṆĀYĀMA), WITH TWO-PART EXHALE

*Note: Although unlikely, if at any time during this exercise your breathing becomes uncomfortable, stop and breathe normally.*

1. Sit as in Position A on the floor or a chair, or lie on the floor or your bed.

POSITION A

2. Take a moment to feel your breath. Notice your body expanding as you inhale and relaxing as you exhale.

3. Imagine a "central channel" running through the center of your body, from the crown of your head to the root at the pelvic floor. This is like a roadway for your attention. Try to follow each breath, from crown to root (top down) on the inhalation as the torso expands, and from root to crown (bottom up) on the exhalation as you pull in the navel. If you get off-track, simply start over.

4. **Over time, bring the inhalation and exhalation to 6–8 seconds each** (modify that number as needed).

5. Next, break the exhalation into two parts as follows:

   - **Inhale** 6-8 seconds. Relax the belly and feel your torso expand.

   - **Exhale** half the breath (about 3–4 seconds) as you contract below the navel.

   - **Hold** for 1–2 seconds, continuing to hold the abdomen in below the navel.

   - **Exhale** the rest of the breath (about 3–4 seconds) as you contract above the navel.

   - **Hold** for 1–2 seconds, continuing to hold the abdomen in above and below the navel.

   - Start over with an inhalation of 6–8 seconds, relaxing the belly and feeling the torso expand.

6. **Continue the two-part exhale practice** for 12 rounds of breath. Pause and notice the effects.

7. Resting Pose (allows the body to absorb the effects of the practice; has a calming and refreshing effect on the energy level)

**8.** Lie in Position A, B, or C. You can also lie on your bed.

POSITION A: RESTING POSE

POSITION B: RESTING POSE, BLANKET UNDER HEAD

POSITION C: RESTING POSE, BLANKET UNDER KNEES

Position your legs a little wider than hip width and your arms about 45 degrees from your body, palms up. Let your feet and legs relax and your fingers curl naturally. **Lie here for 5–10 minutes.** The body and mind benefit greatly from this time to absorb the benefits of the practice. And hopefully you'll soon see the end of constipation!

### OPTIONS FOR SHORTER VERSIONS OF THE "CONSTIPATION PRACTICE"

1. Poses 1–4, 13, 15, 16

2. Poses 1–7, 16

3. Poses 1–3, 7–9, 12, 16

# PRACTICE FOR DEPRESSION

*Suggested time to do this practice: first thing in the morning or early afternoon*

**Bonus:** This practice is also great for getting a good night's sleep!

The yoga therapy approach to addressing depression is with an uplifting theme and energizing postures and breath work, particularly adding a hold after the inhalation. But when you're going through cancer treatment, you may not have enough energy to do an energizing practice! Therefore, do whatever suits you best on the day you do this practice. Doing any sort of practice may help more than doing nothing. You can always calibrate, like reducing the number of repetitions, skipping the hold after inhale, or chanting very softly.

## SET THE THEME

Select an uplifting theme for your practice to address depression. For example, the concept of *light* is an important and often-used image in the yoga tradition. It represents not only the light of the sun, that bright light which energizes us, but also the light of the mind, the flame of knowledge and intelligence, as well as the light within the heart, our inner awareness. It also represents the quality of *lightness*, being light on your feet, light as a feather.

Other themes for addressing depression might be *energy, vitality, strength, joy.* Choose a theme that is personally meaningful to you.

*Write your personal theme here:*

_____

## OPENING

An opening ritual shifts the mindset; it's like a "wake-up" call to the present moment. If you have items on an altar, ring the chime and light the candle and/or incense. Pause to let your senses take in the sound, light, and/or smell.

Sitting on the floor or in a chair, take three simple breaths in and out through your nose. Acknowledge inwardly, *I am beginning my practice now.*

RITUAL IS LIKE A WAKE-UP CALL TO THE PRESENT MOMENT.

BEGIN YOUR PRACTICE WITH INTENTION

## INNER FOCUS

Here you shift attention from external to internal. You can sit or lie down.

1.  Do the steps below with an open mind, not analyzing or judging. This takes practice, so don't worry if your mind feels busy at first. Take a few moments with each step.

    • **Body:** Notice alignment, sensations.

    • **Mind:** Notice thoughts and/or emotions without engaging in the "inner conversation."

    • **Breath:** Notice each breath as it comes in and out through your nose. Make a soft hiss at the throat to slow down and smooth out the breath. On each inhalation, let the torso expand. On each exhalation, gently draw the navel in.

    • **Chant** (Optional): If you like chanting and find that sound vibration lifts your mood or energy, incorporate a chant into your practice. Don't worry about a specific tune; this is just for you. Examples for a depression practice might be: *Let the sun shine; Sun is shining; Joy, joy, joy.*

    • **Chant your word or phrase 3 times.** With a practice for depression, it's ideal to chant out loud and to use a slightly higher pitch to lift your energy. For instance, if you were using the phrase *Sun is shining,* you would:

» Inhale smoothly.

» On exhale, chant out loud **Sun is shining** (make it last about 6 seconds)

- **Reflect** on how your theme may help you. You might ask yourself, *How can the image of sunlight help me today? What light do I need today?* Take a few moments to sit with your question; no need to answer right now.

## MOVEMENT

Now you begin the yoga postures for this practice, shown on the following pages. Be sure to modify the exercises for your needs, or skip those which are not useful or safe for you on any given day.

# 1. TABLETOP/CHILD POSE, WITH OPTIONAL CHANTING

(ARTICULATES THE SPINE, STRETCHES LOWER BACK; CHANTING ENHANCES CONNECTION TO PERSONAL THEME)

1. Begin in Position A.

POSITION A: START HERE

2. **Inhale** and begin to simultaneously lift chest and head, as in Position B.

POSITION B: INHALE TO BEGIN COMING FORWARD

3. Continue the **inhalation** as you come to all fours, chest lifted, as in Position C. Draw the shoulders away from the ears. Avoid overarching the spine. If it's uncomfortable to do one continuous inhalation, just breathe smoothly and naturally.

POSITION C: COMPLETE THE INHALATION HERE

4. **Exhale** and begin to reverse the movement, as in Position D.

*Option:* **Chant on exhalation.**

POSITION D: EXHALE TO BEGIN MOVING BACK

**5.** As you complete the **exhalation**, return to Position A by bowing to the forearms, then lowering the head, and finally settling hips to heels.

POSITION A: COMPLETE THE EXHALATION HERE

**6.** Repeat 3–6 times.

## 2. COBRA POSE (STRENGTHENS UPPER BACK, CORE; LIFTS ENERGY LEVEL)

1. Begin in Position A.

POSITION A: START HERE

2. **Inhale** and traction your palms downward to elongate your chest forward and up, as in Position B. You don't have to lift very high. Use your back muscles to lift your chest, rather than doing a push-up with the arms or pulling up with the head and neck. Gently tighten the legs and buttocks to stabilize your low back.

POSITION B: INHALE TO THIS POSITION

3. **Exhale** to Position A.

4. **Repeat 3–6 times.** Then repeat three times more, remaining in Position B for two rounds of breath each time, before **exhaling** to end at Position A.

# 3. LOCUST POSE (STRENGTHENS UPPER BACK, CORE, BUTTOCKS, LEGS; LIFTS ENERGY LEVEL)

1. Begin in Position A.

POSITION A: START HERE

2. **Inhale** and traction your palms downward to elongate your chest forward and up, and raise the **right** leg, as in Position B. You don't have to lift very high. Use your back muscles to lift your chest, rather than doing a with the arms or pulling up with the head and neck. Lengthen through the lifted leg and squeeze at the crease of the buttock to isolate the working muscles.

POSITION B: INHALE TO THIS POSITION (RIGHT LEG LIFTED)

3. **Exhale** to Position A.

POSITION A: EXHALE TO THIS POSITION

4. **Inhale**, repeat with the **left** leg, as in Position C.

POSITION C: INHALE TO THIS POSITION (LEFT LEG LIFTED)

5. **Exhale** to Position A.

6. **Repeat the sequence 3 times.**

   *Option:* For a more invigorating effect, repeat three times more, remaining in Position B and C for 2 rounds of breath each time, before **exhaling** to end at Position A.

# 4. SWEEPING ARMS/CHILD POSE, WITH OPTIONAL CHANTING (BRINGS CIRCULATION TO UPPER BACK, NECK, SHOULDERS; STRETCHES LOW BACK; STRENGTHENS CORE; CHANTING ENHANCES FOCUS AND CONNECTION TO PERSONAL THEME)

*Caution: Get your doctor's clearance if you have osteoporosis of the spine.*

**1.** Begin in Position A.

POSITION A: START HERE

**2.** On **inhale,** initiate movement between the shoulder blades to begin simultaneously lifting arms, upper back, chest, and head, as in Position B.

POSITION B: INHALE TO BEGIN UPWARD SWEEPING MOTION

**3.** Continue **inhaling** through the upward motion of the arms and body, as in Positions C, D, and E. This should be one smooth motion, with the arms sweeping wide.

POSITIONS C, D, AND E: CONTINUE SWEEPING THE ARMS UP

4. Complete the **inhalation** at the top of the movement, with the arms overhead, as in Position F. If
it's difficult to do one continuous inhalation, just
breathe smoothly and naturally.

POSITION F: COMPLETE THE INHALATION HERE

5. **Exhale** and sweep the arms wide to begin the reverse
movement, as in Positions E, D, C, and B. This
should be one smooth motion. If it's uncomfortable to do one continuous exhalation, just breathe
smoothly and naturally.

*Option:* **Chant on exhalation.**

6. Complete the **exhalation** at Position A.

7. **Repeat the sequence 3–6 times.**

# 5A. MOUNTAIN POSE, HOLD AFTER INHALE AND OPTIONAL CHANTING (STRETCHES FULL BODY; STRENGTHENS LEGS, CORE; BUILDS BALANCE AND FOCUS; LIFTS ENERGY LEVEL; CHANTING ENHANCES CONNECTION TO PERSONAL THEME)

1. Begin in Position A.

POSITION A: START HERE

2. **Inhale** and raise your heels as you sweep your **right** arm up and your **left** arm halfway, as in Position B. It's fine to keep the feet on the floor, as well! **Hold** the breath for 2 seconds after the inhalation. Relax the throat and jaw.

POSITION B: INHALE TO THIS POSITION (RIGHT ARM UP/LEFT ARM HALFWAY; HOLD 2 SECONDS

3. **Exhale** to Position A. Try to coordinate the movement so the arms and heels lands at the same time (but don't worry if that doesn't happen at first!).

4. **Inhale** and raise your heels as you sweep your **left** arm up and your **right** arm halfway, as in Position C. **Hold** 2 seconds after the inhalation.

POSITION A: EXHALE TO THIS POSITION

POSITION C: INHALE TO THIS POSITION (LEFT ARM UP/RIGHT ARM HALFWAY); HOLD 2 SECONDS

5. **Exhale** to Position A.

6. **Repeat the sequence 3 times.**

# 5B. MOUNTAIN POSE, WITH HOLD AFTER INHALE AND OPTIONAL CHANTING

**1.** Begin in Position A.

POSITION A: START HERE

**2. Inhale**, raise your heels and sweep both arms overhead, as in Position B. It's fine to keep the feet on the floor, as well. Hold for 2 seconds in this position and feel the energy you are using!

POSITION B: INHALE TO THIS POSITION; HOLD 2 SECONDS

**3. Exhale** and lower the arms and heels to Position A. Try to coordinate the movement so the arms and heels land at the same time (but don't worry if that doesn't happen at first!)

*Option:* **Chant on exhalation.**

**4.** **Repeat 3–6 times.**

# 6. WARRIOR I, HOLD AFTER INHALE AND OPTIONAL CHANTING (STRENGTHENS LEGS, BACK, SHOULDERS; LIFTS ENERGY LEVEL; CHANTING ENHANCES CONNECTION TO PERSONAL THEME)

1. Begin in Position A.

POSITION A: START HERE

2. **Inhale**, lunge, bending your **left** knee and stretch the arms wide, palms up, as in Position B. Stay grounded through the back foot, leaning your torso forward of the hips, and stretch the chest. Avoid jutting the head forward. **Hold** the breath for two seconds after the inhalation.

POSITION B: INHALE TO THIS POSITION; HOLD TWO SECONDS

3. **Exhale** to Position A.

   *Option:* **Chant on exhalation.**

4. **Repeat for 3 rounds.**

CONTINUED ON NEXT PAGE ↦

**5.** Then **stay** in Position B as you **inhale** and stretch your arms wide. **Hold** for 3–4 seconds after the inhalation.

POSITION B: INHALE IN THIS POSITION;
HOLD 3–4 SECONDS

**6.** **Exhale** and place your hands at the heart, as in Position C.

*Option:* **Chant on exhalation.**

POSITION C: EXHALE IN THIS POSITION

**7.** **Repeat Positions B–C for 3 rounds of breath.**

**8.** **Exhale** to Position A.

**9.** Repeat the entire sequence with the **right** leg forward.

# 7. STANDING FORWARD BEND (COMPENSATES FOR PREVIOUS
## BACK BENDING POSE; STRETCHES BACK OF BODY)

*Caution: If you have low blood pressure, vertigo, glaucoma, go between Position A and C only, keeping your head above your heart. Get your doctor's clearance if you have osteoporosis of the spine.*

1. Begin in Position A. **Inhale** here.

POSITION A: START HERE WITH AN INHALATION

2. **Exhale**, bend your knees slightly and slide your hands down the legs to any comfortable position (Position B). Relax the back of your neck; relax your shoulders away from your ears. Feel your spine gently rounding.

POSITION B: EXHALE TO THIS POSITION.

*Option:* Remain in this position to breathe smoothly for a few rounds of breath.

3. **Inhale** and keep the slight bend in your knees as you lift the chest and head through Position C, pressing up through the legs and feet to stand all the way up to Position A. *(Hint: Think of coming up like a cobra, articulating up through the spine by lifting the chest and upper back first. Avoid "rolling up like a rag doll.")*

POSITION C: INHALE TO BEGIN COMING UP.

COMPLETE INHALATION HERE

4. **Repeat 3–6 times.**

# 8. REVOLVED TRIANGLE POSE (ROTATES SPINE, RIBCAGE, SHOULDER GIRDLE; STRENGTHENS CORE; HAS A REFRESHING EFFECT ON THE ENERGY LEVEL)

*Caution: Skip this pose if it causes or exacerbates shoulder pain or sacrum pain. Get your doctor's clearance if you have osteoporosis of the spine.*

1. Begin in Position A. **Inhale** here.

2. **Exhale** as you take your **left** arm toward your **right** foot, and your **right** arm toward the sky (Position B). The head can be down, sideways, or up, based on your comfort level.

POSITION A: START HERE

POSITION B: EXHALE TO THIS POSITION

**3.** **Inhale** to Position A.

POSITION A: INHALE TO THIS POSITION

**4.** **Exhale** and pull the navel in as you take the **right** arm toward the **left** foot, and the **left** arm toward the sky (Position C).

POSITION C: EXHALE TO THIS POSITION

**5.** **Inhale** to Position A.

**6.** **Repeat the sequence 3 times.**

*Option:* For a more invigorating effect, remain at Position B and C for 2 rounds of breath each time, before **inhaling** to end at Position A.

# 9. CHILD TO TABLETOP TO DOWN DOG, WITH OPTIONAL CHANTING (COMPENSATES FOR PREVIOUS TWISTING POSE; STRENGTHENS ENTIRE BODY; STRETCHES ARMS, SHOULDERS, LEGS, BACK; HAS A REFRESHING EFFECT ON ENERGY LEVEL; CHANTING ENHANCES CONNECTION TO PERSONAL THEME)

**1.** Begin in Position A.

POSITION A: START HERE

**2.** **Inhale** and lift your chest and head, coming to Tabletop position. Draw the shoulders away from the ears. Avoid overarching the spine. At the end of the inhalation, curl the toes under (Position B).

POSITION B: INHALE TO THIS POSITION, CURL TOES UNDER

**3.** **Exhale** and push away from the floor, raising your hips up and letting your head release into Down Dog, as in Position C. Keep a little bend in the knees. Press the hands into the floor. Stretch your tailbone way up; stretch through your armpits!

*Option:* **Chant on exhalation**

POSITION C: EXHALE TO THIS POSITION

**4.** **Inhale** and lift your head and chest as you lower your knees to Position D, uncurling the toes.

POSITION D: INHALE TO THIS POSITION, UNCURL THE TOES

**5.** **Exhale** and reverse the movement back to Position A.

*Option:* **Chant on exhalation.**

POSITION C: EXHALE TO THIS POSITION

**6.** **Repeat the sequence up to 3 times.** Take extra breaths, as needed, throughout the sequence.

*Option:* For a more invigorating effect, stay in the Down Dog position for 2–3 rounds of breath. End in Position A and rest there until your breath is calm.

## 10. SUPINE LEG STRETCH (STRETCHES BACK OF LEGS; IMPROVES CIRCULATION; HAS A REFRESHING EFFECT ON THE ENERGY)

**1.** Begin in Position A.

POSITION A: START HERE

**2.** **Inhale** and extend your legs upward, as in Position B. You can also do this exercise one leg at a time. It's fine if your knees don't straighten all the way. Just stretch comfortably without causing your body to arch up.

POSITION B: INHALE TO THIS POSITION

**3.** **Exhale** to Position A.

**4.** **Repeat 3–6 times.**

*Option:* For a more invigorating effect, hold Position B for 1–3 rounds of breath.

# 11. KNEES TO CHEST POSE, WITH OPTIONAL CHANTING

(GENTLY STRETCHES LOW BACK; MASSAGES COLON; CHANTING ENHANCES
CONNECTION TO PERSONAL THEME)

**1.** Begin in Position A. **Inhale** here.

POSITION A: INHALE HERE

**2. Exhale**, gently draw the navel in as you bring the
knees closer to the chest, as in Position B. Feel
your low back press into the floor.

*Option:* **Chant on exhalation.**

POSITION B: EXHALE TO THIS POSITION

**3.** Repeat 6–8 times.

## 12. RESTING POSE (ALLOWS THE BODY TO ABSORB THE EFFECTS OF THE PRACTICE; HAS A CALMING AND REFRESHING EFFECT ON THE ENERGY LEVEL)

1. Lie in Position A, B, or C. You can also lie on your bed.

POSITION A: RESTING POSE

POSITION B: RESTING POSE, FOLDED BLANKET UNDER HEAD

POSITION C: RESTING POSE, ROLLED BLANKET UNDER KNEES

2. Position your legs a little wider than hip width and your arms about 45 degrees from your body, palms up. Let your feet and legs relax and your fingers curl naturally. **Lie here for 5–10 minutes.** The body and mind benefit greatly from this time to absorb the benefits of the practice.

# BREATH PRACTICE (PRĀṆĀYĀMA)

1. Sit, as in Position A. You can also sit in a chair or lie on the floor or your bed.

POSITION A

2. Take a moment to feel your breath. Notice your body expanding as you inhale and relaxing as you exhale.

3. Imagine a "central channel" running through the center of your body, from the crown of your head to the root at the pelvic floor. This is like a roadway for attention. Try to follow each breath, from crown to root (top down) on the inhalation as the torso expands, and from root to crown (bottom up) on the exhalation as you pull in the navel. If you get off-track, simply start over.

4. Once you've established that pattern of following the breath with your attention, begin the following set of breaths, modifying as needed:

   » **Inhale** 6 seconds; **Hold** 2 seconds; **Exhale** 8 seconds - *for 4 rounds*

   » **Inhale** 8 seconds; **Hold** 2 seconds; **Exhale** 10 seconds - *for 4 rounds*

   » **Inhale** 8 seconds; **Hold** 4 seconds; **Exhale** 10 seconds - *for 4 rounds*

   » **Inhale** 6 seconds; **Hold** 2 seconds; **Exhale** 8 seconds - *for 2 rounds*

5. Then allow the breath to return to its natural rhythm.

# MEDITATION

You may choose to simply sit in stillness, experiencing the effect of your breath practice.

Or, you may want to use the "Cave of the Heart" visualization. This is a yoga practice of meditation in our deepest heart. Take some time with each of these steps below.

1. Tune into the effects of your practice. Feel the circulation in your body from the movement and breath work. Feel a sense of peace after unplugging from the mind's ongoing chatter.

2. Picture yourself in the cave of your heart. Everyone pictures this special place differently, and whatever image appears is the right one. It might be a forest path, or a quiet beach, a mountain vista, or something else entirely.

3. Focus on the quality embodied by your personal theme. Sense this quality streaming from the top of your head, down the central channel, into the cave of your heart where you are seated. For example, if you selected

*Sunshine*, sense or feel *Sunshine* flowing down through the central channel, filling your heart and from there, flowing through your entire body. Actively focus on that quality for several minutes. Feel that you are absorbing that light and, with it, that quality of your theme.

4. Now allow yourself to feel an awareness of depression. Maybe in this quiet state you can greet the depression, acknowledge it, and perhaps see it not as part of you, but as a state you've been in or an experience you've had, like a weather front that has stalled. From within your deepest heart, recognize that, like the weather, all transient states change. And *you* are separate from all transient states. You are unchanging.

5. Recognize your own inner light; feel it in your own way. Reassure yourself that you have the capacity for inner strength, energy, and joy, despite external conditions. Actively focus on acknowledging and feeling those qualities for several minutes.

## CLOSING

When you sense yourself coming out of the meditative state, repeat or chant your theme three times (once silently, once softly, and once more loudly) to symbolize returning from the inner world to the outer. If you have altar items, extinguish the candle and ring the singing bowl. Listen until the soft vibrating chime has completely dissipated.

You may want to jot a few notes in a journal about your experience with the practice. I found it very helpful to put things into words. This brings purpose and intention to your practice and to your commitment to your well-being.

## OPTIONS FOR SHORTER VERSIONS OF THE "PRACTICE FOR DEPRESSION"

1. Opening; Inner Focus; Poses 1–6; Breath Practice; Meditation

2. Opening; Inner Focus; Poses 4–10; Breath Practice; Meditation

3. Opening; Inner Focus; Poses 1–4, 7-11, 13; Breath Practice; Meditation

# SAMPLE PRACTICE FOCUSING ON THE CROWN CAKRA (*SAHASRĀRA*)

*Suggested time to do this practice: any time of day is fine,*
*but early morning or before bed are especially nice.*

The crown cakra is called *sahasrāra* (pronounced suh HUSS raara—both r's are slightly rolled) in Sanskrit. The word means *thousand-spoked* and refers to a symbolic lotus flower said to sit above the head like a crown. *Sahasrāra* represents an opening to that which is beyond the mind, where we might merge with sources of inspiration.

The *Cakra* Model is a symbol system for describing the movement of energy through our body and its effect on our multidimensional nature (remember the Five Aspects Model). That's a huge simplification of a complex topic! For our purposes, we want to use components of the *Cakra* Model that are relevant to our current situation in order to create a helpful practice. I chose the crown *cakra* because so much of what I've shared with you in this book has been about recognizing conditioned responses and transient states of mind and finding ways to shift beyond those mindsets.

## THEME

The theme for our crown *cakra* practice is **opening to sources of inspiration.**

## OPENING

An opening ritual shifts the mindset; it's like a "wake-up" call to the present moment. If you have items on an altar, ring the chime and light the candle and/or incense. Pause to let your senses take in the sound, light, and/or smell.

Sitting on the floor or in a chair, take three simple breaths in and out through your nose. Acknowledge inwardly, *I am beginning my practice now.*

BEGIN YOUR PRACTICE WITH INTENTION

## INNER FOCUS

Here, you shift attention from external to internal.

1. Do the steps below with an open mind, not analyzing or judging. Take a few moments with each step.

   • **Body:** Notice alignment, sensations.

LIE DOWN OR SIT COMFORTABLY

   • **Mind:** Notice thoughts and/or emotions without engaging in the "inner conversation."

   • **Breath:** Notice each breath as it comes in and out through your nose. Make a soft hiss at the throat to slow down and smooth out the breath. On each inhalation, let the torso expand. On each exhalation, gently draw the navel in.

   • **Chant:** *Oṁ*

     » Inhale smoothly.

     » On exhale, chant *Oṁ*, letting the syllable last for six seconds. You don't need to stretch it out until you are completely out of breath! Finish with the "mmm" sound as your lips come together.

> » Repeat 3 times.

- **Reflect** on how the theme may help you. You might ask yourself, *How can opening to something beyond me help today? What sources of inspiration do I need today?* Take a few moments to sit with your question; no need to answer right now.

## A NOTE ABOUT CHANTING OṀ:

The syllable and the sound *Oṁ* represent the part of us that is pure consciousness. The term *pure consciousness* is an attempt to articulate something that is all but impossible to convey in words. It evokes that which is highest for you, the practitioner. It may come from your spiritual tradition or from an individual sense of transcendence. You can substitute any word or phrase that speaks to you personally at the level of inspiration—*Amen, Truly, Holy, Olam, Ahad.* (For a reading suggestion on *Oṁ*, see Resources at the end of the book.)

## MOVEMENT

Now you begin the yoga postures for this practice, shown on the following pages. Be sure to modify the exercises for your needs, or skip those which are not useful or safe for you on any given day.

# 1. MOUNTAIN POSE, HOLD AFTER INHALE AND OPTIONAL CHANTING (STRETCHES FULL BODY; STRENGTHENS LEGS, CORE; BUILDS BALANCE AND FOCUS; LIFTS ENERGY LEVEL; CHANTING ENHANCES CONNECTION TO THEME)

**1.** Begin in Position A.

POSITION A: START HERE

**2.** **Inhale**, raise your heels and sweep both arms overhead, as in Position B. It's fine to keep the feet on the floor, as well. **Hold** for 2 seconds in this position and feel the crown of the head.

POSITION B: INHALE TO THIS POSITION; HOLD 2 SECONDS WITH ATTENTION AT CROWN

**3.** **Exhale** and lower the arms and heels to Position A. Try to coordinate the movement so the arms and heels land at the same time (but don't worry if that doesn't happen at first!)

*Option:* Chant a 6-second *Oṁ* on exhalation.

**4.** Repeat 3–6 times.

# 2. STANDING FORWARD BEND (STRETCHES ENTIRE BACK OF BODY)

*Caution: If you have low blood pressure, vertigo, glaucoma, go between Position A and C only, keeping your head above your heart. Get your doctor's clearance if you have osteoporosis of the spine.*

1. Begin in Position A. **Inhale** here.

POSITION A: START HERE WITH AN INHALATION

2. **Exhale**, bend your knees slightly and slide your hands down the legs to any comfortable position (Position B). Relax the back of your neck; relax your shoulders away from your ears. Feel your spine gently rounding.

POSITION B: EXHALE TO THIS POSITION.

*Option:* Remain in this position to breathe smoothly for a few rounds of breath.

3. **Inhale** and keep the slight bend in your knees as you lift the chest and head through Position C, pressing up through the legs and feet to stand all the way up to Position A. *(Hint: Think of coming up like a cobra, articulating up through the spine by lifting the chest and upper back first. Avoid "rolling up like a rag doll.")*

POSITION C: INHALE TO BEGIN COMING UP.

COMPLETE INHALATION HERE

4. **Repeat 3–6 times.**

## 3. REVOLVED TRIANGLE POSE (ROTATES SPINE, RIBCAGE, SHOULDER GIRDLE; STRENGTHENS CORE; HAS A REFRESHING EFFECT ON THE ENERGY LEVEL)

*Caution: Skip this pose if it causes or exacerbates shoulder pain or sacrum pain. Get your doctor's clearance if you have osteoporosis of the spine.*

1. Begin in Position A. **Inhale** here.

POSITION A: START HERE

2. **Exhale** and take your **left** arm toward your **right** foot, and your **right** arm toward the sky (Position B). The head can be down, sideways, or up, based on your comfort level.

POSITION B: EXHALE TO THIS POSITION

**3.** **Inhale** to Position A.

**4.** **Exhale** and take the **right** arm toward the **left** foot, and the **left** arm toward the sky (Position C).

POSITION A: INHALE TO THIS POSITION

POSITION C: EXHALE TO THIS POSITION

**5.** **Inhale** to Position A.

**6.** **Repeat** the sequence 3 times.

CONTINUED ON NEXT PAGE ⇗

**7.** Then **exhale** to Position B.

POSITION B: EXHALE TO THIS POSITION

**8. Inhale** and stretch **right** arm forward, looking toward the hand, as in Position D.

POSITION D: INHALE TO THIS POSITION

9. **Exhale** and draw elbow back, looking toward the floor, as in Position E.

POSITION E: EXHALE TO THIS POSITION

10. **Repeat Positions D–E 3 times.**

11. Then **repeat Positions D-E** on opposite side of body.

# 4. TABLETOP/CHILD POSE, WITH OPTIONAL CHANTING

(ARTICULATES THE SPINE, STRETCHES LOWER BACK; COMPENSATES FOR PREVIOUS TWISTING POSTURE; CHANTING ENHANCES CONNECTION TO THEME)

1. Begin in Position A.

POSITION A: START HERE

2. **Inhale** and begin to simultaneously lift chest and head, as in Position B.

POSITION B: INHALE TO BEGIN COMING FORWARD

3. Continue the **inhalation** as you come to all fours, chest lifted, as in Position C. Draw the shoulders away from the ears. Avoid overarching the spine. If it's uncomfortable to do one continuous inhalation, just breathe smoothly and naturally.

POSITION C: COMPLETE THE INHALATION HERE

4. **Exhale** and begin to reverse the movement, as in Position D.

*Option:* Chant a 6-second *Oṁ* on exhalation.

POSITION D: EXHALE TO BEGIN MOVING BACK

5. As you complete the **exhalation**, return to Position A by bowing to the forearms, then lowering the head, and finally settling hips to heels.

POSITION A: COMPLETE THE EXHALATION HERE

6. Repeat 3–6 times.

## 5. BRIDGE POSE (STRENGTHENS LEGS, HIPS, CORE; ARTICULATES THE SPINE; STRETCHES THE CHEST AND UPPER BACK)

1. Begin in Position A.

POSITION A: START HERE

2. **Inhale**, press your feet into the floor and raise the pelvis to Position B. Rest on your upper back and shoulders, *not on your neck*. Squeeze the buttocks for stability.

POSITION B: INHALE TO THIS POSITION

3. **Exhale**, gently draw the navel in and lower the spine vertebrae by vertebrae to Position A. Try to keep a backward pelvic tilt all the way through the exhale movement so the lower spine rolls onto the mat as you come down.

4. **Repeat 3–6 times.**

# 6. SEATED TWIST, WITH OPTIONAL MENTAL CHANTING

(MASSAGES THE COLON; ROTATES THE SPINE; STRENGTHENS THE CORE; HAS A REFRESHING EFFECT ON THE ENERGY LEVEL, CHANTING ENHANCES CONNECTION TO THEME)

*Caution: Avoid this pose if you have osteoporosis of the spine.*

1. Begin in Position A, right hand on left knee, left hand on floor behind the body. **Inhale** here.

POSITION A: START HERE WITH AN INHALATION

2. **Exhale** and twist to the **left,** as in Position B.

POSITION B: EXHALE TO THIS POSITION

3. **Inhale** to Position A.

4. **Repeat 3 times.**

5. Then **stay** in Position B for three rounds of breath, holding your attention at the crown of head.

*Option:* **Mentally chant a 6-second *Oṁ* on each exhalation.**

6. Repeat entire sequence to opposite side (Positions C-D).

POSITION C: INHALE IN THIS POSITION

POSITION D: EXHALE IN THIS POSITION

7. **Inhale** to Position A to end.

# 7. KNEES TO CHEST POSE, WITH OPTIONAL CHANTING
## (GENTLY STRETCHES LOW BACK; MASSAGES COLON)

1. Begin in Position A. Let your feet and legs relax; the arms do the work in this pose. **Inhale** here.

POSITION A: INHALE HERE

2. **Exhale**, gently draw the navel in as you bring the knees closer to the torso, as in Position B. Feel your low back press into the floor.

   *Option:* Softly chant a 6-second *Oṁ* on exhalation.

POSITION B: EXHALE TO THIS POSITION

3. **Repeat 6–8 times.** Make your breath and movements flow together smoothly.

# 8. RESTING POSE (ALLOWS THE BODY TO ABSORB THE EFFECTS OF THE PRACTICE; HAS A CALMING AND REFRESHING EFFECT ON THE ENERGY LEVEL)

1. Lie in Position A, B, or C. You can also lie on your bed.

POSITION A: RESTING POSE

POSITION B: RESTING POSE,
FOLDED BLANKET UNDER HEAD

POSITION C: RESTING POSE,
ROLLED BLANKET UNDER KNEES

2. Position your legs a little wider than hip width and your arms about 45 degrees from your body, palms up. Let your feet and legs relax and your fingers curl naturally. **Lie here for 5–10 minutes.** The body and mind benefit greatly from this time to absorb the benefits of the practice.

## BREATH PRACTICE (PRĀṆĀYĀMA)

1. Sit, as in Position A. You can also sit in a chair or lie on the floor or your bed.

POSITION A

2. Take a moment to feel your breath. Notice your body expanding as you inhale and contracting as you exhale.

3. Imagine a "central channel" running through the center of your body, from the crown of your head to the root at the pelvic floor. This is like a roadway for your attention. Try to follow each breath, from crown to root (top down) on the inhalation as the torso expands, and from root to crown (bottom up) on the exhalation as you pull in the navel. If you get off-track, simply start over.

4. Once you've established this pattern of following the breath with your attention, **silently chant a 6-second *Oṁ* with each inhalation and exhalation for 9 rounds** (gradually work up to 12 rounds). You can keep track by touching your thumb to successive fingertips. If your mind wanders, just bring it back.

## MEDITATION

You may choose to simply sit in inner stillness, focusing on the soft, natural flow of your breath.

Or, you may want to use the "Cave of the Heart" visualization that I used. This is a yoga practice of meditation in our deepest heart. Take some time with each of the steps below.

1. Tune into the effects of your practice. Feel the circulation in your body from the movement and breath work. Feel a sense of peace after unplugging from the mind's ongoing chatter.

2. Picture yourself in the cave of your heart. Everyone pictures this special place differently, and whatever image appears is the right one. It might be a forest path, or a quiet beach, a mountain vista, or something else entirely.

3. With an open mind, consider your true sources of inspiration. Consider how you conceive of "that which is beyond the mind" and how you connect to that transcendent quality. Stay detached from editorializing or explaining.

4. Ask for help to open up to this dimension, to be able to tap into those deep sources of inspiration.

5. Imagine that source of inspiration streaming like sunlight from the top of your head,

down the central channel, into the cave of your heart where you are seated. Actively focus on that quality for several minutes. Feel it in your own way.

6. Recognize your potential for connecting to that which is highest for you, to sources beyond the mind, pure inspiration, pure consciousness. Pause in the experience of being merged with that same consciousness.

### CLOSING

When you sense yourself coming out of the meditative state, **chant a 6-second *Oṁ***, once silently, once softly, and once more loudly, to symbolize returning from the inner world to the outer. If you have altar items, extinguish the candle and ring the singing bowl. Listen until the vibrating chime has completely dissipated.

You may want to jot a few notes in a journal about your practice. I found it very helpful to put things into words. This brings purpose and intention to your practice and bolsters your commitment to caring for yourself.

### OPTIONS FOR SHORTER VERSIONS OF THE "CAKRA PRACTICE"

1. Opening; Inner Focus; Poses 1, 2, 4; Breath Practice; Meditation

2. Opening; Inner Focus; Poses 5, 6, 7; Breath Practice; Meditation

# RESOURCES

## PREFACE

*Yoga Therapist Directories:*

- Viniyoga: Viniyoga.com/directory
- Other traditions: https://yogatherapy.health/find-a-therapist/

## CHAPTER 4: ALTAR-ED REALITY

- Ganesh invocation: Returnyoga.org
- Yoga mat reviews for Lululemon, Jade, and Yoga Accessories: https://www.nytimes.com/wirecutter/reviews/best-yoga-mats/

## CHAPTER 11: WHAT GOES UP

- Yoga for depression workshop with Gary Kraftsow of the American Viniyoga Institute: https://viniyoga.com/shop/ecourses/yoga-therapy-for-depression/
- Yoga for depression practice (DVD or digital download) with Gary Kraftsow of the American Viniyoga Institute: https://viniyoga.com/shop/video/dvd-viniyoga-therapy-for-depression/

## CHAPTER 15: APPLY AND REAPPLY

- Lavender Healing Salve, available online at Lancaster Farmacy: https://www.lancasterfarmacy.com/product-page/healing-salve-1
- Vicco Turmeric Skin Cream (cooling skin cream)
- Miaderm Radiation Relief Cream

## CHAPTER 16: RECOVERY MARATHON

*Cakra Model*

- Kabel, O. (2015, June 3). "The Chakra model: The yogic map of personality." SequenceWiz. https://sequencewiz.org/2015/06/03/the-chakra-model-the-yogic-map-of-personality/

## CHAPTER 19: CATCH AND RELEASE

- Barnes Method Myofascial Release Therapist Directory: myofascialrelease.com/find-a-therapist

## CHAPTER 22: PRACTICES

### Teachings on Oṁ

- Swami Rama, *Oṁ, the eternal witness: Secrets of the mandukya upanisad* (Lotus Press, 2007).

## GENERAL

### Information, Education, Resources on Cancer

- American Cancer Society: https://www.cancer.org/

### Research on Yoga and Cancer

- *International Journal of Yoga Therapy*: https://yogatherapy.health/research/

## YOGA THERAPY

- Gary Kraftsow, *Yoga for transformation: Ancient teachings and practices for healing the body, mind, and heart* (Penguin Publishing, 2002).

# NOTES

## PREFACE

1. Juliana Steele, *Laughing All the Way* (Juliana Steele, 2019).

## INTRODUCTION

1. "Viniyoga," accessed November 2024, https://viniyoga.com/.
2. "About Gary Kraftsow," accessed November, 2024, https://viniyoga.com/about/gary-kraftsow/.

## CHAPTER 2: ARE YOU AFRAID I'LL DIE?

1. Swami Rama, Rudolph Ballentine, MD, Alan Hymes, MD, *Science of Breath: A Practical Guide* (Himalayan Institute, 1998), 63-4.
2. Gary Kraftsow, *Yoga for Transformation* (Penguin Compass, 2002), 120-21.

## CHAPTER 3: IT'S JUST PRACTICE

1. Pandit Rajmani Tigunait, PhD, *The Practice of the Yoga Sutra* (Himalayan Institute, 2017), 14.

## CHAPTER 5: I'M POSITIVE

1. "Ornish Lifestyle Medicine," accessed November 2024, http://ornish.com/.
2. "Dr. Rick Hanson," accessed November 2024, https://rickhanson.net.
3. Diane Serra et al., "Outcomes of guided imagery in patients receiving radiation therapy for breast cancer," Clin J Oncol Nurs., Dec;16(6) (2012): 617-23, doi: 10.1188/12.CJON.617-623. PMID: 23178354.
4. David Bresler, "Physiological Consequences of Guided Imagery," Pract Pain Manag, 2005;5(6), https://www.medcentral.com/pain/chronic/physiological-consequences-guided-imagery.
5. Richard Davidson and Sharon Begley, *The Emotional Life of Your Brain* (Plume, imprint of Penguin Books, 2013).
6. "Dr. Rick Hanson," accessed November 2024, https://rickhanson.net.
7. Ranju Roy and David Charlton, *Embodying the Yoga Sutra* (Weiser Books, 2019), 14-29.

## CHAPTER 6: LET'S GET THE CHEMO SHOW ON THE ROAD

1. https://en.wikipedia.org/wiki/Desiderata

## CHAPTER 7: HELLO, NAUSEA. HOW ARE YOU TODAY

1. Thich Nhat Hanh, *Peace is Every Step, The Path of Mindfulness in Everyday Life* (Random House, 1992), 51-67.

## CHAPTER 8: EXERCISING MY RIGHTS

1. "For Women with Breast Cancer, Regular Exercise May Improve Survival," NIH, May 15, 2020, https://www.cancer.gov/news-events/cancer-currents-blog/2020/breast-cancer-survival-exercise.
2. Jessica M. Scott et al., "Timing of exercise therapy when initiating adjuvant chemotherapy for breast cancer: a randomized trial," Eur Heart J, 2023 Dec 7;44(46):4878-4889, Doi: 10.1093/eurheartj/ehad085.
3. Elizabeth Miller, "Prayer, Medical Science and Cancer" (Newsletter: Religion in American Life, Fall 1997).
4. Herbert Benson, and Marg Starg, *Timeless Healing* (Scribner 1997).

## CHAPTER 11: WHAT GOES UP

1. "depression," *Merriam-Webster.com,* accessed November 2024, https://www.merriam-webster.com/dictionary/depression.
2. Thich Nhat Hanh, *Peace is Every Step, The Path of Mindfulness in Everyday Life* (Random House, 1992), 51-67.
3. "Dr. Rick Hanson," accessed November 2024, https://rickhanson.net.
4. "Positive thinking: Stop negative self-talk to reduce stress," Mayo Clinic, Nov. 21, 2023, https://www.mayoclinic.org/healthy-lifestyle/stress-management/in-depth/positive-thinking/art-20043950.
5. "About Kristine Kaoverii Weber," accessed November 2024, https://subtleyoga.com/kristine-kaoverii-weber/.
6. Ay Atezaz Saeed et al., "Depression and Anxiety Disorders: Benefits of Exercise, Yoga, and Meditation," *Am Fam Physician*, 2019 May 15;99(10):620-627. PMID: 31083878.

7. Gary Kraftsow, *Yoga for Transformation* (New York: Penguin Compass, 2002), 120-21.

### CHAPTER 12: ROCKY, DON'T YOU FORGET ABOUT ME

1. Shankar Vedantam, podcast host, "You 2.0: The Mind's Eye," *Hidden Brain*, hiddenbrain.org, August 10, 2020, accessed November 2024, https://hiddenbrain.org/podcast/you-2-0-the-minds-eye/.

### CHAPTER 14: COOL, COOL, COOL

1. Diane Serra, et al., "Outcomes of guided imagery in patients receiving radiation therapy for breast cancer," *Clinical Journal of Oncology Nursing*, 2012 Dec; 16(6):617-23. doi: 10.1188/12.CJON.617-623.

2. Cortland J. Dahl et al., "The plasticity of well-being: A training-based framework for the cultivation of human flourishing," Proc. Natl. Acad. Sci. U.S.A., 2020, 117 (51) 32197-32206, https://doi.org/10.1073/pnas.2014859117.

3. Loren Toussaint et al., "Effectiveness of Progressive Muscle Relaxation, Deep Breathing, and Guided Imagery in Promoting Psychological and Physiological States of Relaxation," Evid Based Complement Alternat Med. 2021 Jul 2;2021:5924040. doi: 10.1155/2021/5924040.

4. Richard Davison et al., "Alterations in Brain and Immune Function Produced by Mindfulness Meditation," *Psychosomatic Medicine* 65(4):p 564-570, July 2003, *DOI:* 10.1097/01.PSY.0000077505.67574.E3.

### CHAPTER 19: CATCH AND RELEASE

1. "The John F. Barnes Myofascial Release Approach," accessed November 2024,  https://myofascialrelease.com.

### CHAPTER 21: HOW YOGA KEEPS HELPING

1. Swami Yogakanti, *Sanskrit Glossary of Yogic Terms* (Bihar School of Yoga, 2007).

# INDEX

# ACKNOWLEDGEMENTS

I started writing this book after receiving a gift from my massage school friends. It inspired me to start journaling, and things took off from there. Thank you all, especially Lianna, Crystal, and Millie.

Thank you, Donna, Philip, and Niles from my writing group for reading many pages and offering your candid, thoughtful feedback. Without the structure and encouragement of a writing group, I'm not sure I would have dived into this project on my own. Thank you, as well, to Pam Seelig for talking with me about her experiences writing and publishing her book about bringing the Yoga Sutras into personal practice.

Along the way, several people read and reread pages to help ensure the book made sense and communicated its message clearly. Heartfelt thanks to Sue, Lynn, Donna, and Liz.

Thanks to Aggie Stewart for copyediting, indexing, and proofreading the manuscript. You turned it into a professional work ready for publication! Thanks to Robin Locke Monda for designing the book cover and the Five Aspects graphic, and Steve Kuhn for designing and formatting the book.

I owe so much to my publishing mentor (and freshman-year roommate!), Lynn. A successful writer herself, she graciously guided and encouraged me through all the steps it took to transform words on a screen into a full-fledged book, and did it with a sense of humor and a bright smile. Lynn, we should have known when we coordinated those matching striped comforters for our dorm room that there was collaboration in our future. Many, many thanks!

I am grateful to all the medical professionals who have treated me over several years. It's not hyperbole to say that together you saved my life. I thank you from the bottom of my heart.

Thank you to my dear friends who visited, grocery shopped, dropped off meals, sent cards and gifts, texted, and called while I was going through treatment. Thank you, Sue, for your weekly handmade cards and for the soft hats you knitted for me—it was a blessing to receive all that love! Thank you, Cherri, for your many cards, touching base in a loving, quiet way and reminding me that you were keeping me in your thoughts. Thank you, Kristin, for reaching out and supporting me, even while your family was going through so much, as well. Thank you, Maureen, Lisa, Robyn, Leslie, Sally for your visits, walks, dinners, wishes, and love. You kept me connected to my "local life," even when I needed to hang out by myself on the couch. And thank you to every single person who mailed a card or sent a text. You have no idea how much those sweet messages meant to me.

I thank Dave, for teaching me so much about myofascial release and energetic bodywork, which have helped transform my inner state, both myofascially and spiritually. The conversations and laughter during our countless appointments (including one during an earthquake!) are special medicine to me.

I want to thank so many yoga colleagues for years of collaboration, friendship, and encouragement. Thank you, Mary Hilliker and Sue Tebb for reading the manuscript and offering your much-appreciated endorsements. Thank you, Kristine Weber, for your insights about how we might forge a more holistic approach to mental health through the tradition of yoga. Thank you, Alex, Margy, Kenneth, Robin, Martha, Shoba, and every student at American Viniyoga Institute whom I've been privileged to work with. I wish I could list every single name here, but that would get tedious, and even those of you whose name would be included would get bored reading through the list! I thank you.

The credit for the basis of this book, yoga as an aid during cancer treatment, goes to my teacher, Gary Kraftsow, and to his teachers, T.K.V. Desikachar and T. Krishnamacharya. Through these inspired teachers, I've learned the profound effect yoga practice can have on me, from my anatomy to my physiology to my inner mind and heart. I truly can't thank them enough for the education I've received about how to understand and apply the tools of yoga. In particular, Gary has given me the gift of context for observing and interpreting the tradition passed on to him by his teachers. He has shown me how to make ancient practices relevant for me, and has bestowed the encouragement to share that with others, as well. Thank you, Gary.

Most especially, I thank my family. You were so vitally important to me during treatment time, although your support then was no different than it is at any time—complete and unconditional. I thank my daughter Emma and my son Michael for accompanying me to chemo, which I'm sure was a little scary and weird. For hanging around with me at home, checking on me by phone, and simply being who you are, the best son and the best daughter ever, as I've explained to you many times! I thank Grace, for your steady love and support. For arranging your schedule to make every one of my chemo appointments. For dropping by to bring me a hamburger or just visit for a little while. Your constancy in my life is a treasure. Thanks to my more-than-a-step-dad, Eddie, and his wife, Cindy, and family, and my sisters Hillary and Chrissy, for texts, calls, visits and love. Thank you to my wonderful cousins Audrey and Curt, and to Aunt Mary for your love and prayers—they were felt from across the miles as if you were right there with me.

And of course, endless thanks to Andy. You've had several loved ones who have experienced cancer, and you've gone through it with them. When I told you I had cancer, you jumped into action, accompanying me to appointments, researching countless details, moving in with me when I needed you most, offering as much of yourself as you could possibly give. I felt completely safe, supported, and bolstered by your unwavering commitment and your cheerful outlook. I can't imagine what it would have been like without you. In fact, because of you, it wasn't that bad! I love you and thank you over and over.

# ABOUT THE AUTHOR

In 1988, **Julie Shaw** had back pain from her long commute to work as a corporate trainer. She looked up "yoga" in the yellow pages and stepped into a lifelong practice. After 15 years as a student, she agreed to teach a couple friends what she knew about yoga. Ten years later she became a certified yoga therapist, using the tools of yoga to help people stay healthy and to manage the symptoms that come along with health conditions. She has worked in hospital settings, physician practices, yoga studios, community settings, and in private with individuals. She is a certified Viniyoga Therapist [AVI®] and has a Master's Degree in Adult Education from Rutgers University. In addition to practicing yoga, Julie loves hiking, gardening, twirling the baton, reading, and correcting other people's grammar, which she is working on overcoming, especially after writing this book and realizing she may not have all the right answers after all.

www.ingramcontent.com/pod-product-compliance
Lightning Source LLC
Chambersburg PA
CBHW041509120626
46551CB00018B/2361

* 9 7 9 8 9 9 0 9 5 7 1 0 7 *